SIX LATVIAN POETS

SIX LATVIAN POETS

Translated, edited
and introduced by

Ieva Lešinska

with
'A Brief Introduction to Latvian Poetry'
by Juris Kronbergs

2011

Published by Arc Publications
Nanholme Mill, Shaw Wood Road
Todmorden, OL14 6DA, UK
www.arcpublications.co.uk

Design by Tony Ward
Printed by Lightning Source

ISBN: 978 1906570 39 2

The publishers are grateful to the authors and,
in the case of previously published works, to their publishers
for allowing their poems to be included in this anthology.

The cover painting is by Juris Petraškevičs,
by kind permission of the artist .

The publication of this book was supported by a grant from the
Latvian Literature Centre and the State Culture Capital Foundation.
The publishers would like to express their gratitude for this support,
without which this book could not have been published.

The 'New Voices from Europe and Beyond' anthology series is published in
co-operation with Literature Across Frontiers which receives support
from the Culture programme of the EU.

Arc Publications 'New Voices from Europe and Beyond'
Series Editor: Alexandra Büchler

CONTENTS

AGNESE KRIVADE

MARTS PUJĀTS

MĀRIS SALĒJS

KĀRLIS VĒRDIŅŠ

Six Latvian Poets is the eighth volume in a series of bilingual anthologies which brings contemporary poetry from around Europe to English-language readers. It is not by accident that the tired old phrase about poetry being 'lost in translation' came out of an English-speaking environment, out of a tradition that has always felt remarkably uneasy about translation – of contemporary works, if not the classics. Yet poetry can be and is 'found' in translation; in fact, any good translation reinvents the poetry of the original, as long as the translator engages in the "perilous business" of translating, as the as Ieva Lešinska, the editor and translator of this volume, puts it, in an effort to "close the substantial distance that separates the Latvian and English languages and overcome the suspicion that what has been said so well in one language cannot possibly be said equally well in another". Translation then becomes the outcome of a dialogue between two cultures, languages and different poetic sensibilities, between collective as well as individual imaginations, conducted by two voices, that of the poet and of the translator, and joined by a third interlocutor in the process of reading.

And it is this dialogue that is so important to writers in countries and regions where translation has always been an integral part of the literary environment and has played a role in the development of local literary tradition and poetics. Writing without reading poetry from many different traditions would be unthinkable for the poets in the anthologies of this series, many of whom are accomplished translators who consider poetry in translation to be part of their own literary background and an important source of inspiration.

While the series 'New Voices from Europe and Beyond' aims to keep a finger on the pulse of the here-and-now of international poetry by presenting the work of a small number of contemporary poets, each collection, edited by a guest editor, has its own focus and rationale for the selection of the poets and poems. In this, the second anthology in the series introducing contemporary Baltic poetry, we meet the younger generation of Latvian poets who started writing and publishing after the country regained independence following the disintegration of the Soviet Union of which it had been part for close to half a century, a generation whose poetics is placed in a wider context by the editor and translator Ieva Lešinska and by a leading poet and translator of the older generation Juris Kronbergs. Their superbly informative introductions offer many insights, both serious and witty, into the present and past of Latvian poetry. I would like to thank them and all the others who made this edition possible.

Alexandra Büchler

EDITOR'S / TRANSLATOR'S PREFACE

In the 1970s, the *grand maître* of Latvian poetry, Knuts Skujenieks, suggested that Latvian poetry, while acknowledging contemporary global trends now and then, stays true to its basic roots in the Latvian folksong (*daina*) tradition, echoing pre-Christian animism and pantheism and "reflecting basic values: concern for the Latvian land and the fates of its people". This remained more or less true into the early 1990s, even past the brief period of patriotic fervour associated with the restoration of Latvian independence and was mostly upheld by the older generation and those few middle-aged poets who, as Jānis Peters put it, were "drafted into the revolution". The new generation of poets, who came of age after 1991 when Latvia resumed its existence as an independent country after a gap of five decades under Soviet rule, however, departed from this tradition. An overt engagement with history or social issues is almost totally absent from their work – perhaps because of an instinctive fear that the weight of history may turn out to be too much to bear and may squash their own creativity, perhaps because of a desire to place themselves in the broader context of world literature or simply because of a youthful opposition to their predecessors. Be that as it may, they are in the process of developing a new language (languages?) for Latvian poetry which will mature in unpredictable ways.

The audience for poetry has also changed immeasurably. In the Soviet period, poetry books were *de rigueur* in any educated Latvian's bookcase. The books came out in editions of ten to twenty thousand and often disappeared into avid readers' hands within hours of release. Poetry, with its highly metaphoric approach to reality, simply could tell stories and express thoughts that were barred from literal expression in the public arena. It was one of the few refuges from the mind-numbing ideology and oppressive banality of Soviet life. As elsewhere in Eastern Europe, poets were respected and revered as bards or even oracles, keepers of the pure essence of the nation. Today, depending on one's age and temperament, one looks upon these times with disbelief and perhaps even a bit of wistfulness. The market for poetry books is moderate at best, with only a few titles published each year. The audiences have shrunk considerably. Yet poetry is far from dead or even ailing in Latvia. Poetry Days, launched in 1965 to commemorate the hundredth anniversary of Rainis, arguably, the greatest Latvian poet, are not only taking place every year but have acquired a much more youthful spirit, with poetry being read not only beside staid monuments to past glory but on street corners, in old factories and warehouses. That venerable West European and North American institution, the book-café, has finally arrived in Riga and is obviously here to stay, with a number of venues for poets to read their work, meet their audiences (mostly young), and hear their colleagues. There is even a book-hair-stylist's shop slightly outside the centre of town in an area that is turning into a haven of alternative culture, the so-called "Republic of Miera Street". Poets are a visible presence at various art and multimedia events. In addition to the single Latvian literary magazine, *Latvju Teksti*, many publish on the Internet – either in their own blogs or at *¼ Satori*, "a Website for Culture and Independent Thought", which is particularly popular among the thirty-something crowd. They are young, bold and uninhibited, they do not need any institution's approval, and many shun even the increasingly geriatric Writers' Union, which used to be a venerable institution wherein membership signified quality achievement and which, after the Stalin era, acted as a self-appointed mediator between the Soviet authorities and Latvian intellectuals. Dismissed as obsolete by many of the younger writers, it has for years been struggling to find its place in a free market economy.

In other words, these days, there seems to be no other reason for writing poetry than the intimate pleasure of writing it, and it is only those for whom it is an important part of their being who stay with it.

While very different poetically, the six poets represented in this anthology, have much in common. They all currently reside in the country's capital, Riga. They are relatively young, their ages spanning the decade between thirty and forty, and they make their living at some other occupation while retaining a serious commitment to poetry or, at least, the written word. Every book they have published and every one of their public readings has generated much interest on the part of the reading public and critics alike. They have been short-listed for or received the top literary prizes awarded in Latvia yet have retained their ability to surprise and their disdain for pandering to any convention or fleeting fashion.

At forty, the most senior among them, Māris Salējs, is arguably the most traditional of the six. As his colleague Kārlis Vērdiņš puts it, the presence of nature in Salējs's poems is "so deeply felt and emotional that [it] becomes an expression of the movements of the poet's active, searching soul: forest, branches, roots, cherries, glowworms and other simple yet capacious facts of reality form mysterious combinations" that they hint at some intuited higher plane. In this, Salējs pays his respects not only to the Latvian tradition (including its twists and bends at the hands of the living Latvian classics, Knuts Skujenieks, Jānis Rokpelnis, and Uldis Bērziņš) but also to the Polish poets from the first half of the twentieth century whose translations formed the bulk of his first book *Māmiņ, es redzēju dziesmu* (Mummy, I Saw a Song, 1999), which was illustrated by the author (he holds a degree in art).

In his second book, *Mana politika* (My Politics, 2001) Salējs further solidifies his poetic outlook, abandoning elements of his earlier at times childlike intonation yet losing none of the emotional directness with which he addresses his reader. A very prolific author, with many published examples of his own original poetry and translations, Salējs modestly claims to find his "own eyes, ears, and voice" only on occasion. Yet his third book is a long awaited event that will no doubt be of consequence for the Latvian poetry scene.

The publication of Anna Auziņa's third book, *Es izskatījos laimīga* (I Looked Happy, 2010) was also long-awaited and most of the poems in this anthology have been drawn from it. The distance – professional, emotional – between her first two books, *Atšķirtie dārzi* (Opened Gardens, 1995) and *Slēpotāji bučojas sniegā* (Skiers Kissing in the Snow, 2001) and the latest one is best described in her own words:

> It seems that in Latvia I am considered the nice, lovable, sincere, and childish poetry girl. My third collection may seem to be more melancholic and bitter. When I started writing poetry I was much influenced by twentieth-century French poetry, particularly that of Saint-John Perse. But speaking of my early poems, it is difficult for me to believe that it was me who wrote them. If before (in creating my first two books) I wrote as naturally as I draw breath, owing everything to what I have in the way of talent and intuition, these days I give much more thought to what I am doing.

The poetic 'I' in *Es izskatījos laimīga* is a mature woman who often finds the most mundane and supposedly "unpoetic" features of life fascinating and exciting, yet who also sees the world as complicated and sad, being familiar as she is with the ambiguities of love – not only for one's partner but also for one's children and friends. The precision of Auziņa's visual observation – she is a professional, exhibiting artist –, the sensuality of her imagery and her experiments with form, however, are clear indications that the playfulness and the sheer joy of poetry so exuberantly present in her earlier work have not been left far behind.

Another poet with three very different poetry books to his name (in addition to a volume of children's poetry, which also caught the attention of many mature readers, receiving Latvia's highest literary award in 2007), Kārlis Vērdiņš, is one of the most outstanding poets of the generation that started publishing in the mid-1990s. At ease with traditional versification schemes, a master of the sheer flow of a poetic phrase and adept at echoing Latvian classics, Vērdiņš never loses his modern sensibility and urban sophistication. Thoroughly steeped in the modernist perspective and aesthetic, he uses the quotidian to express the noble and vice versa, and always succeeds in offering the reader a new perspective. He uses irony and even sarcasm, yet his voice, never shrill, somehow retains real warmth. This intonation lends itself well to music, which explains why Vērdiņš is the author of lyrics for a number of musical compositions, from popular songs to music for plays and opera. The expressiveness of his poetry owes much to Latvian modernists who emigrated, as political refugees, to the United States at the end of the Second World War and formed a group called Elles ķēķis (Hell's Kitchen), as well as to his close reading of such English language poets as Shakespeare, Emily Dickinson, D. H. Lawrence, T. S. Eliot, H. D., E. E. Cummings, and many others. A skilful translator of Russian poetry, Vērdiņš, along with all the other poets in this anthology, maintains close ties to the Orbita group of poets writing in Russian, participating in their multimedia projects and in the friendly practice of mutual translation. If part of the appeal of Vērdiņš's first book, *Ledlauži* (Icebreakers, 2001) was its open same-sex eroticism (a first in Latvian literature), with his second book, *Biezpiens ar krējumu* (Cottage Cheese with Cream, 2004), Vērdiņš had definitely established himself as a mature poet in full control of his talent, one who cannot be tied down to any one genre, agenda, or social group, and so bold as to challenge his readers anew with a third book frankly entitled *Es* (I, 2008) that begins by deliberately misquoting Rainis in its epigraph. The fact that Vērdiņš manages to elegantly combine a Ph.D. in literature with mean riffs on the guitar (playing with the 'poets' band' Maukas (Sluts)) is alone an indication of this poet's range.

A more serious musician and a more irreverent poet is Marts Pujāts, the only one among the six who is still under thirty. Upon graduating from the Riga Dom Choir School, that rigorous institution for talented young musicians where he was taught musical composition by, among others, the internationally acclaimed Pēteris Vasks, he published his first book of poetry *Tuk tuk par sevi* (Knock Knock for Myself, 2000) at the tender age of eighteen. The book revealed a landscape that seemed to fit the post-modernist world, yet contained many a beast and vegetable hitherto unknown in Latvian poetry while at the same time offering a fresh and youthfully sincere perspective. Unlike the rest of the poets featured in this book, Pujāts's fresh and youthful perspective seems to reject the Latvian poetic tradition altogether. His is a fragmented reality where words, chosen with unmistakable precision, seem to acquire new, pure expression and energy that seems to strive toward some inscrutable absolute. "I am an anti-song", he claims, while clearly confident of the unmistakable song present in his poetry. That presence becomes overt in his second book, aptly titled *Mūsu dziesma* (Our Song, 2008). On the back cover of the book, Kārlis Vērdiņš issued this passionate recommendation:

> Subject this book to long and careful reading, read it through several times. Quote on your blog and in conversations with colleagues the lines that you like the best. Learn at least one poem by heart. If you know any foreign language, translate a few of the poems. Give a copy of this book to your high-school literature teacher.

While it is not clear if many teachers of Latvian literature have been the lucky recipients of Pujāts's book, students should certainly watch out for his name to appear on future required reading lists.

Ingmāra Balode and Agnese Krivade chose to play with the concept of childhood in their debut books (both came out within a short time of each other in 2007), which are entitled *Ledenes, ar kurām var sagriezt mēli* (Bonbons That May Cut Your Tongue) and *Bērnība* (Childhood), respectively. Krivade, whose book has been designed to look like a girl's scrapbook held together by a pretty ribbon, sees the concept through to the end and, as some critics put it, with a kind of 'in-your-face' aggression. If it can really be called that, this is the aggression of someone always trying to tell the truth, someone principled and youthfully allergic to compromise. Tension, however, is created by the sheer talent evident in the poetry, talent that tones down the truth Krivade's protagonist seeks, and brings it to a more human scale. Childishness appears mainly in poems where Krivade abandons herself to the language, acceding to something quirky, accidental, playfully improvisational. The poet herself says that "language in a good part of the poems is intended to be vernacular. Whatever is said, is said as if without thinking, just fooling around. [...] The rhythms form as if by accident, as if on second thought." What she is trying to represent is perhaps not so much her own childhood as the way people talk about childhood:

> I have noticed that in any social situation people become childish as soon as the topic of childhood is brought up. Everyone is eager to share his or her adventures and emotions, highlighting the importance of their own childhood. They tend to forget the rules of adult conversation and may not even wait till the other person has finished their story. My book *Childhood* seemed to me one of the more legitimate ways of talking about all kinds of my firsts, although it may be a bit impudent, given that a book on childhood is usually one of the last books in any author's life.

Given the popularity of Krivade's writings of all kinds, her readers are hoping to see much more in the way of poetry. I know this reader is.

Just like Agnese Krivade, Ingmāra Balode wears many hats (artist, journalist, editor, manager of cultural projects), yet that of a poet seems to be the most evident and fitting. Her first book, while very different from Krivade's, shares with it a yearning for purity not easily found in urban life, yet the intonation is calmer, perhaps more resigned. Balode's imagery, while appealing to the senses, is sometimes difficult to decipher. Her poems seem to shield themselves from any facile intellectual analysis, yet their inherent music is unmistakable and draws one in almost in spite of oneself, injured "tongue" or not. She sometimes uses words and phrases that in less skilful hands would seem hackneyed treacle, but in her poetry seem fresh and surprising as if she was the first to speak them. At the same time, she is equally at home in the modernist paradigm (laconic expression, no punctuation, unusual phrasing), showing influences of her experience in translating twentieth and twenty-first century poetry, ranging from e.e. cummings to Adam Zagayewski. As critic Anna Millere wrote on the *¼ Satori* website, Balode's poetry "may not reveal anything new, yet it dares to uncover and explore the existing forms – both poetic structures and the world and the ways it is experienced." When Balode is at her best, her poetry seems to be unfolding in real time, as if it were composed before our very eyes.

If I am permitted a subjective note, I have to admit that I like all six. I look forward to reading their work as it appears in the printed and electronic media, not least because it often challenges my poetic sensibilities. I enjoy being surprised by the modulations of their strong, youthful voices and always want to hear and read more. They make me feel like engaging in the perilous business of translating: to try to close the substantial distance that separates the Latvian and English languages and overcome the suspicion that what has been said so well in one language cannot possibly be said equally well in another. In that sense, this book is a labour of love, with no less emphasis on labour than on love.

Of course, there are many other good poets in Latvia, some of whom I have translated, some that I hope to translate in the future. Yet these six seem to be most rapidly approaching the peak of their craft. I cannot wait for what they will have to say once they have got there.

Ieva Lešinska

A BRIEF INTRODUCTION TO LATVIAN POETRY

> *"Today it would be truly difficult to find another nation in Europe that so rightfully deserves to be called the nation of poets; it would be equally difficult to find another country that deserves to be called the land of poetry as much as the homeland of the Latvians... Every Latvian is a born poet, they all compose verses and songs, and they can all sing these songs."*
>
> (German geographer and traveller J. G. Kohl, 1841)

First, a few words about why the British readers *should not* get interested in Latvian poetry. They should have no interest in Latvian poetry just because there are cheap Ryanair flights from London to the 1679 km distant Riga, cheap beer, or because Latvia has defeated Great Britain in basketball five out of six matches, with the last an 86 / 84 victory at the "Efes Pilsen" world cup championship in Ankara; or because Churchill said in 1946 that from "the Baltic to [...] the Adriatic an iron curtain has descended" across Europe. Nor should they care for Latvian poetry just because the influential political philosopher Sir Isaiah Berlin was born and spent his childhood in Riga; or because Alfred Hitchcock in the role of a diplomat in one of his movies says: "I speak Latvian". And certainly not because in the 1920s and 1930s Britain was the biggest market for Latvian bacon and butter. No, the British reader should learn about Latvian poetry because it stands on its own two feet, offering the English-speaking reader its own peculiar aesthetics, world view, and a lyricism that is rooted in the old Latvian folksongs and winds like a red thread through Latvian poetry irrespective of the sometimes extremely trying political circumstances and a variety of literary "-isms" up to our time. For Latvian poets, poetry has always been a "serious game".

Since Latvia regained independence in 1991, its publishing industry has experienced a quantum leap. Hundreds of optimistic publishers have flooded the market, some only managing to publish a single book. In 2009, 529 first editions of prose and poetry were released in Latvia. Of those, 209 were original Latvian works, among them 126 poetry titles with an average print run of 1000 copies. Latvia's population is currently about 2.3 million, of which about 1.5 million read Latvian literature (given that Britain's population is about 61 million, that is about forty times that of Latvia, one would imagine that about 5000 new poetry titles come out in Britain every year, with an average print run of 40,000!).

Latvian Poetry in English

The most frequently checked-out book in the collection of the Stanford University library in the late 1960s was a translation of Latvian folk-poetry entitled *Sex Songs of the Ancient Letts* translated by Bud

Berzing, *pseud.* (New York: University Books, 1969). This certainly seems to have been the most famous book of translated Latvian poems ever to appear at a single time and place. The very first English translations of Latvian folk poetry, however, appeared in the *Foreign Quarterly Review* (1831) authored by Sir Walter Scott. The first anthology, *The Tri-Colour Sun* (Cambridge University Press) was published in 1936. It was compiled by its translator, W. K. Matthews, who taught the English language and literature at the University of Latvia in Riga in the period between the two world wars. 1957 saw the publication of a revised and updated version of this book under the title *A Century of Latvian Poetry* (London: John Caldar, 1957). Unfortunately, both in terms of the selection of poems and quality of the translations, the anthology left much to be desired.

Folk-poetry: the Dainas

No one knows just how old the Latvian folksongs are. All we know is that the first written versions date back to the early seventeenth century. Despite their great age, however, they have not been outdated: immediate and topical, ideologically they could have been written just outside Woodstock at the end of the 1960s. Their message is ecological, anti-war and matriarchal. They follow a person from the cradle to the grave, maintaining that people and nature are interdependent and the natural world should therefore be treated with respect and care. They celebrate the festivals of the agricultural year and encompass an extensive pre-Christian mythology. Closer to the precepts of Buddhism than of Christianity, their short form and laconic imagery seem akin to haiku. This oral tradition was kept alive in the main by generations of women and we don't know how far back in time it stretches, though some say it is as old as the Latvian language itself.

This folksong tradition had already come under attack from thirteenth century invaders of the territory that later became Latvia. Known as the Teutonic knights, they came swinging a sword in one hand and the Bible in the other so as to conquer and Christianize the people. Despite this, and the subsequent disparagement of the folksongs on the part of the Lutheran Church and the local representatives of the German Enlightenment, the oral tradition persisted and developed. But it was only in the nineteenth century that the scholar Krišjānis Barons collected, collated, collocated and published 239.000 Latvian folksong quatrains in six volumes (1894-1905). It was from Volume 6 that our North American friends (possibly young second-generation American Latvians) got their erotically-charged songs. The folksong tradition has been maintained as a living tradition to this day, and by 2000, the Archives of Latvian Folklore contained

1,043,841 numbered folksong quatrains.

Latvian folk poetry developed along with and reflects the development of the Latvian language. Interestingly, we cannot find in its original sources something corresponding to the ubiquitous conjunction *un*: it was borrowed later from German (*und*), whereas diminutives are used much more widely than today, implying not only a small size but a psychological attitude: intimacy, irony, or respect, depending on the context.

The Language

That we can still read and understand these centuries old folksongs without any difficulty has to do with the how relatively few fundamental changes the Latvian language has undergone over time. Latvian is a synthetic language, which can cause certain difficulties in translating poetry into the analytic English. Synthetic languages tend to be more concise and less wordy, as the prefixes, suffixes, and grammatical endings carry meaning and the word order is not very rigid. For example, "The dog bit the man" in Latvian would be "Suns iekoda vīram". Inverting the sentence – "The man bit the dog" – radically changes the situation whereas in Latvian "man" and "dog" can be casually replaced by one another – "Vīram iekoda suns" – while preserving the meaning. That meaning is safely guarded by the noun endings that can be relied upon to inform us exactly who bit whom. This opens great possibilities for the poet. It is also an important reason why the main issue for Latvian poetry is "how it sounds" and not "what it means" which seems to be the main concern of poetry in English.

The Origins of Latvian Poetry

In feudal times, the first texts printed in the Latvian language were a result of the competition between Catholicism and Lutheranism in the sixteenth century: religious texts, hymns, psalms, the Lord's Prayer, sermons, and the first Latvian phrase book. A Polish-Latin-Latvian dictionary appeared in 1681 and in 1694 the publishing of the Bible in Latvian was sponsored by the Swedish King Carl XI. The first Latvian Grammar, which devoted a whole chapter to folksongs, appeared in 1761. At the same time, philosopher Johann Gottfried Herder, for some years a German pastor in Riga, included Latvian folksongs in his *Stimmen der Völker in Liedern* and formulated his idea of national identity through language and traditions. Sir Walter Scott must surely have used his translations in German when he translated some of them into English.

Despite this interest in the Latvian language and Latvian folkloric traditions in certain enlightened circles, the conventional wisdom that dominated in the ruling classes for many centuries was that an educated person could not be a Latvian. The peasant population, in fact, did not even have a national denomination of their own – they were simply called *die Un-Deutsche* (Non-Germans). Their language was said to be incapable of expressing thoughts of any complexity and their folksongs were just scurrilous ditties and vestiges of ancient superstition or erotically charged vulgarisms.

After the Great Nordic War, Latvian literature stagnated until the mid-eighteenth century when G. F. Stender the Elder published his work. His didactic psalms were not much loved, as opposed to his *Holy Stories* (1757, later also called the *Little Bible*). Each story ended with a synopsis of the main points in the form of a ditty: Stender took the spiritual development of the common folk to heart. People liked them and even passed them on from generation to generation.

Stender's poetry covered the main genres of his era: it was pseudo-classicist, sentimental, and didactic. Failing to share in the budding interest in the folksongs, he wanted to replace them with his moralizing verse that lent itself well to oompah-accompaniments. In this he had many followers up until the mid-nineteenth century. Many of his poems were about love: he wanted to provide more "tasteful" alternatives to the erotic folksongs where, in Stender's opinion, the sexual motifs appeared in a fashion that was too open and lewd. Despite all these drawbacks, his poetry was not without its merit, for it ploughed an unchartered territory.

In the second decade of the nineteenth century, serfdom was abolished in Livonia and agrarian law made it possible for Latvians to buy property and achieve a better standard of living. Latvian city dwellers became a factor in Latvian development and opportunities for Latvian parents to educate their children became more readily available. The first Latvian newspaper, *Latviešu Avīzes* (Latvian Gazette), started publishing in 1822. 1856 saw the launch of *Mājas Viesis*, a magazine that became a forum for the so-called Young Latvians, a place where they could voice their concerns and opinions, all directed at the expansion of political, economic, and intellectual rights for the Latvian population.

The father of Latvian drama and one of the most important authors of the novella genre was Rūdolfs Blaumanis, 1863-1908. An excellent lyricist, he was also an important commentator on social issues as can plainly be seen in his satirical and humorous verse. In his time, writing poetry was such a popular pastime that Blaumanis felt compelled to ask whether and how a Latvian could possibly avoid this preoccupation:

> (...) If we take a closer look at this matter, we have to recognize that it really is not easy not to become a poet. It takes a very strong charac-

> ter to be able to resist. It is a misconception that one is protected by having no talent. Talent is a secondary matter. It would be an exaggeration to claim that it is outright harmful, but it would be a blatant lie to assert that it is indispensable. There are of course people that can refrain from writing poetry only by not being born. (...) It is my belief that our young people should be forbidden to read literary compositions. Yet that would hardly suffice. We should start with somehow scaring our children away from poetry. Perhaps we could use horror stories in which a poet is featured as a ghost or with stories where he is the butt of jokes. More well-to-do families should try to bribe some gaunt, dirty, and shaggy person who every once in a while is presented as a poet, setting an appalling example for children. If the child would not listen, try to use threats: 'Just you wait, if you don't behave, a poet will come and take you to the forest!' In addition, children should be taught to respect money and be told that all poets, and especially Latvian poets, tend to die of hunger.

No research has been done to find out to what extent parents followed Blaumanis's recommendations, but there has been no dearth of poets since his time.

'The Awakening'

Published in 1856, the same year that Baudelaire's *Les Fleurs du mal* initiated European poetic modernism, a book appeared that is widely held to mark the real beginning of Latvian poetry: it was called *Songs*, a collection mainly of translations by Juris Alunāns who set out to refute the parochial prejudices of his time. Alunāns wanted to prove that both philosophical thought and subtle emotion could be expressed in Latvian. Around this time, one that in Latvia is called 'The Awakening' (but elsewhere in Europe is referred to simply as Nationalism), the Young Latvians launched a trend devoted to the appreciation of the glorious Latvian past, including the folksong tradition. A motley crew of national romanticists appeared writing poetry of uneven quality, the first song festival was held and there were also a series of teachers' conferences where demands for greater rights of access to the Latvian language in schools were made (one must remember that Latvia was far from being an independent state at this time: in fact, it was a province of the Russian Empire). These were the heady years that also produced the cornerstone of Latvian fiction *Mērnieku laiki* (Times of the Surveyors, 1879) by the Kaudzīte Brothers with its vivid descriptions of country life and its social strata.

The New Current

A few years later, around the turn of the century, the national romantic urge to find an idyllic Latvian past had run its course. Industrialization and the urbanization policies of the modernizing Russian regime replaced it with a politically left-leaning New Current that appealed to many young poets also. Eduards Veidenbaums, 1867-1892, was among the most talented.

Despite the fact that he did not write much – his legacy consists of seventy-five poems and less than two dozen translations (of Horatio, Schiller, Heine) – Veidenbaums was a truly fresh and interesting voice in Latvian poetry. A student of law in Tartu (Dorpat), he was also interested in history, philosophy, politics, and foreign languages, acquiring a good working knowledge of Russian, German, French, English, Italian, Spanish, Estonian, Greek, Latin, and Hebrew. Despite his avowed interest in the Classics, particularly Horatio, he was one of the founders of a literary society whose members were budding Marxists. Veidenbaums studied forbidden Marxist literature and wrote an essay on class contradictions in Latvia. His social concerns are also reflected in some of his poetry where he uses satire, irony, and sarcasm to criticize the social inequality and unjust political order of his day. Yet other poems show him as a lone and pessimistic seeker at times claiming that life has no purpose and at other times praising a carpe diem approach to life. Demonstrating a remarkable facility with the poetic form, he still felt that content should take precedence and poetry should primarily serve a social instead of a purely aesthetic function. Veidenbaums's social pathos made him very popular among the progressive youth of Latvia, with his peers copying and illegally disseminating his poems. Because of a strict censorship under the tsar, the corpus of Veidenbaums's poetry could be published only many years after his death from tuberculosis just short of twenty-five years of age.

After the failed revolution of 1905 and the tsarist revenge, many writers who had been active during the uprising were forced to seek political asylum abroad. That was the first emigration of intellectuals from Latvia, including a married couple, Jānis Rainis and his wife Aspazija, both of whom were poets and playwrights, and the most prominent of them all.

Aspazija (*nom de plume* of Elza Rozenberga), 1868-1943, won critical and popular acclaim with her first book of poetry, *Sarkanās puķes* (Red Flowers, 1897) where she expressed her disdain for the limits of day-to-day existence, praising life of the spirit and romantic love. Her next book, *Dvēseles krēslā* (Soul's Twilight, 1904) was full or melancholy and sympathy for the revolutionaries that were imprisoned or exiled. Throughout her career as a poet, Aspazija was preoccupied with perfecting her individual consciousness, registering the various states of her psyche. In 1905, her plays, for example *Sidraba šķidrauts* (The Silver Veil) and *Atriebēja* (The Avenger) played a significant role.

Upon returning from his law studies in St. Petersburg, Rainis (real name Jānis Pliekšāns), 1865-1929, became editor-in-chief of the newspaper *Dienas Lapa* (Daily Page) which, under his guidance, acquired an increasingly Marxist slant. 1897 saw the publication of his translation of Goethe's *Faust*, which is considered an important contribution to the development of the Latvian language: many of the words he borrowed from archaic and dialectal sources as well as his neologisms became a mainstay of the modern Latvian language. During the revolution of 1905 Rainis was among the leading organizers and agitators. When the uprising was defeated, he and Aspazija escaped to Switzerland. A very prolific writer and translator, Rainis's produced collected works that comprise two dozen volumes: poetry, drama, letters, and diaries. The most important of his translations include the works of Pushkin, Lermontov, Shakespeare, Schiller, Heine, Lessing, Hauptmann, Ibsen, Calderon, Alexander Dumas père, and Lord Byron.

For fifteen years Rainis and Aspazija lived in Castagnola, near Lugano. On the beautiful mountain slopes leading to Lake Lugano, the socialist Rainis was the first to formulate the idea that, instead of a part of a democratic Russia, Latvia should become an independent country. The years of exile turned out to be very productive for Rainis: he composed several important poetry collections where he ruminated on the failure of the revolution of 1905 and incorporated Eastern philosophies and Tagore's style in his own work. Subsequently his poetry was used for ideological purposes both by the Soviet communists and the nationalists in exile. Many Latvians know some of his poems by heart, but it is his plays that seem more important in today's cultural context. Strangely enough, his exile writings, with some exceptions, were permitted by censorship to be published in Riga, that is in tsarist Russia, the very empire he was fighting. 1920 saw Rainis and Aspazija's triumphal return to the newly independent Latvia.

Jānis Poruks, 1871-1911, kept his distance from the New Current and its socialist ideals. He believed that any individual should rid themselves of selfishness and strive for ever greater humanism and compassion. The ideals of Hernhutism inherited from his parents played a major role in his world view. A student of music in Dresden, he devoted more of his time to German literature and the philosophy of Nietzsche. Well versed in the European literature of his time, he nevertheless maintained close ties to the Latvian individualist poetry and national romanticism of the 1880s. His novel contribution to Latvian poetry was his keen interest in the conflicts of thought, feeling, and passion along with his attempts to find a synthesis between the three.

So far then we have folk poetry, this inexhaustible source of inspiration to poets, composers, and artists and the substantial work done by the first Latvian poets in proving to themselves and others that, to quote the Swedish poet Sonnevi, “we are not shit”. Their quest to establish the Latvian identity culminated in the revolution of 1905 and then in the independence proclamation of 1918. The groundwork was laid, and the accomplishments, moderate as they might seem, were enough to serve as a trampoline for later generations of poets whose work could compete with the world’s best. Most important, perhaps, is the fact that poetry meant so much to the entire nation.

Decadents

Symbolism or Decadence entered Latvia through Russia. Viktors Eglītis, 1877-1945, who was a friend of the Russian poet Valery Briusov, showed himself as a decadent with his book *Elēģijas* (Elegies, 1907), later becoming the leader of the Latvian decadents. Just like his spiritual forebears, Edgar Allan Poe, Baudelaire, and Maeterlinck, he was interested in exploring the dark forces inhabiting the human psyche with the help of deeper symbolism. Another notable decadent was Fallijs, 1877-1915, whose experimental poetry often broke with conventional syntax, highlighting the Dionysian elements, particularly sexual in nature, reaching a high level of cultural synthesis. The Decadents thought very highly of themselves and tended to publish admiring articles about each other. Fallijs took the praise very seriously: in one of his poems he calls himself “an immortal spirit of song” declaring that he is standing “alone on the edge of a precipice” and predicting that “even my foe will mourn my passing”. This era saw the emergence of a variety of literary newspapers that tended to criticize each other, often by means of vitriolic poetry.

A translator of French poetry, Edvarts Virza, 1883-1940, had great facility with the poetic form. In his first book of erotic poetry he is close to the Decadents, but in later years it turns to rather exalted expressions of patriotism and love for his native area; his most famous work, the prose poem ‘Straumēni’ is composed in the same vein.

First World War, Independence and Modernism

The First World War resulted in a collapse of the great empires and the emergence of new, independent countries, Latvia among them. During the war, most of the large factories and their equipment were evacuated from Riga to Russia; a substantial number of the Latvian Riflemen chose to remain in communist Russia, poets among them. They even established a Latvian publishing house, Prometejs, in Moscow. Many of the revolutionaries of 1905, however, participated in fighting for Latvia’s freedom: the so-called “battles for freedom” lasted until 1920.

Kārlis Skalbe, 1879-1945, was one of the freedom fighters. After his active participation in the revolution of 1905, he was forced to go into exile, first to Switzerland and then to Finland and Norway. Upon his return, he was sentenced to one and a half years in prison. Skalbe spent the war years as a war correspondent, actively fighting against tsarist rule in Latvia. His poetry and particularly his fairy-tales are popular to this day. At the end of the Second World War Skalbe again went into exile and died in Stockholm that same year.

Like Skalbe, Linards Laicens, 1883-1938, also took part in the revolution of 1905 and supported the idea of independence, but in 1920 he became a communist, moving to the Soviet Union in 1932. Six years later he fell victim to the purge of 1938, meeting the fate of the majority of Latvians living in Russia who were shot or sent to the Gulag in 1937; having no one left to publish, Prometejs also ceased to exist. Posthumously rehabilitated in the post-Stalinist era, Laicens is mostly remembered for his books of poetry, *Karavane* (Caravan, 1920) and *Ho-Taī* (1922) that include both ideologically charged and lyrical poems; in *Ho-Taī* he successfully applied forms borrowed from Chinese poetry.

If the failed revolution of 1905 ploughed the soil for disappointment, melancholy, and escapism, the First World War spawned Expressionism. One of the first and most important Expressionists in Latvian poetry was Jānis Sudrabkalns, 1894-1975. His first book of poetry, *Spārnotā armāda* (The Winged Armada, 1920) expressed humanist and pacifist ideas and testified to its author's optimism about the future. His second volume, *Spuldze vējā* (Light-bulb in the Wind, 1931), by contrast, is full of bitterness and pain. Under the *nom de plume* Olivereto, Sudrabkalns published several collections of satirical poems. After the establishment of Soviet power in Latvia, he became something of a court poet, tirelessly singing praises of the régime, never again betraying the lyrical subtlety or acerbic wit of his earlier career. Eriks Ādamsons, 1907-1946, found his inspiration in English and Scottish poetry. A consummate aesthete, Ādamsons wrote poetry that made ample use of classically pure form.

Aleksandrs Čaks, 1901-1950, a contemporary of both Ādamsons and Sudrabkalns, was the most influential among the Modernists. He spent the war years and some of the postwar period in Russia where he heard Mayakovsky read his poetry. "I observed him with the curiosity of a boy staring at a big new automobile", he later wrote. Mayakovsky and Yesenin, as well as diligent studies of Latvian poetry, were the life sources of Čaks's own. Having returned to Latvia in 1922, his début in 1928 caused a sensation. After his first volumes, *Es un šis laiks* (I and This Time) and *Sirds uz trotuāra* (Heart on the Pavement), the books which followed a year later – *Pasaules krogs* (World Pub) and *Apašs frakā* (Apache in Tails) – made him wildly popular. To those critics who bemoaned his pessimistic outlook he replied: "With their pessimism the young poets want to open the modern man's eyes so that he can see the rotting puddle of society in which he is reclining so comfortably." Čaks's poetry is full of extravagant comparisons and metaphors. He keeps the reader riveted by the vivid scenery, the wealth of personification, wild imagination, and the very expressiveness of his language. His poetry offers a gateway to both the later poets and those who claim not to be interested in poetry. With his vitality, multi-layered and surprising – yet at the same time accessible – metaphors and comparisons, he opens the door to the human world of fantasy and emotion. In 1938 Čaks published his long poem *Mūžības skartie* (Touched by Eternity), dedicated to the Latvian Riflemen who fought for "a free Latvia within a free Russia" during the Russian revolution. After the Second World War, however, the poem was banned in Soviet Latvia for its "narrow-minded nationalism". During the height of Stalinism, Čaks felt compelled to write poetry flattering to the powers that be. An aficionado of his poetry once told me that she had expressed her outrage at this way of degrading himself as a poet; Čaks had looked at her wistfully and said: "Don't you worry, little girl, when the times change, so will the poems." The lyrical strand of Latvian poetry is not absent even from Čaks's most modernist, futurist poems. Arguably, he may be the gentlest of the European futurists of the time. His influence on Latvian contemporary poetry is greater than any other poet's.

The Second World War and After – Emigration

The Second World War and its aftermath split the Latvian poetry in three: some of the poets found themselves in the Gulag, others went into exile in the West, the third, largest group, remained in Latvia. The Western literary life (about 300,000 Latvians ended up in the West) was very active: in addition to publishers, there were also literary magazines of which *Jaunā Gaita*, which, established in the mid-1950s in the United States, eventually moved to Canada and has enjoyed an uninterrupted existence to this day. The Latvian modernism, launched by Čaks, continued in the West. In Stockholm, where many cultural figures had found refuge and established newspapers and publishing ventures, Dzintars Sodums, 1926-2007, published his poetry that was in opposition to the nostalgically patriotic poetry of the established exile poets. In the 1950s young poets established an informal group called Elles Ķēķis (Hell's Kitchen) in New York, with Gunars Saliņš, 1924-2010, and Linards Tauns, 1924-1963, as its leading voices. Los Angeles and London were the new-found homes to the only notable Beat generation poet, Olafs Stumbrs, 1931-1996, and the creator of "movement poetry" and yoga teacher, Velta Sniķere, b. 1920, who to this day accompanies her poetry readings with illustrative movements.

Gunars Saliņš's writing is anchored in the poetry of Čaks and Rilke and T. S. Eliot alike and is inspired by modern art as a whole. His collection *Melnā saule* (Black Sun) features various reminiscences, allusions, dedications, and descriptions of bohemian gatherings. His very precisely drawn verbal canvases do not preclude free travel between reality and dreams, the present and the past. The intense feeling evoked by New York co-exists with remembered landscapes from the poet's childhood: thus, cows may suddenly appear on the streets of the American metropolis.

Sweden provided shelter to Veronika Strēlerte, 1912-1993, poet and translator from French. Her intellectual poetry is replete with quiet lyricism; her very first collection, *Vienkārši vārdi* (Simple Words, 1937), was marked by a remarkable control of form and rich vocabulary. Classical in spirit, her poetry reached toward clarity, combining cool observation with the symbolism that accompanies deep feeling. In her later writing, she turned to free verse.

The Soviet Period

In Soviet occupied Latvia, just like elsewhere in the Soviet Union, the 1956 Communist Party Congress and Khruschev's speech revealed to the world Stalinist crimes against humanity and became a watershed event that allowed many to return from exile in Siberia. A more liberal era set in for poetry. The late 1950s saw the débuts of three outstanding poets: Ojārs Vācietis, 1933-1983, Imants Ziedonis, b. 1933, and Vizma Belševica, 1931-2005. Just like Yevgeni Yevtushenko and Andrei Voznesensky in Russia, they became very popular, their poetry readings drawing huge audiences. This was a time for literature in disguise: poetry was the medium for secret messaging between lines, conveying what was not possible to convey in any other way. Poetry played a multifaceted role, substituting for what in the Western democracies was taken for granted: freedom of the press and religion, of thought and expression. Yet the fight with the Soviet censorship was constant and, in Belševica's case, rather brutal. Her book of poems *Gadu gredzeni* (Rings of Years, 1969) was printed and available in bookstores when some vigilante noticed that some of the poems in it seemed to be directed at the powers that be, for example, 'Indriķa Latvieša piezīmes uz Livonijas hronikas malām' (Notes of Henricus Lettus on the Margins of the Chronicle of Livonia). As the title suggests, superficially the poem told the story of German crusaders and the violent and deceitful measures they took to baptize the Baltic heathens, as well as expressing contempt for those among the locals who served them, yet when asked if perhaps the poem was really about contemporary Latvia, Belševica answered in the affirmative. The book was withdrawn from circulation and the poet accused of "pseudo-modernist tendencies" and a "narrow, philosophically erroneous interpretation of history". She was banned from publishing for seven years but by the early 1980s she had become a virtual non-person: her name did not appear anywhere as if she had ceased to exist.

The treatment of Knuts Skujenieks, b. 1936, by the Soviet authorities was even harsher: in 1962, during Khruschev's "thaw", he was sent to one of the Gulag camps in Mordovia. Why? The official reason was his refusal to inform on his fellow citizens, with the exacerbating factor of owning a set of *Encyclopedia Britannica*. Years later Skujenieks said, without a trace of irony, that he is grateful to the Gulag for it made him into a poet: in the camp, poetry was not just a pastime but a life principle for him. Over the seven years of imprisonment, Skujenieks wrote more than a thousand poems. Sent out in letters to loved ones, carried out surreptitiously, every single one has survived yet they were published in a book only after the collapse of the Soviet Union. Written in the camp, they are not about the camp: Skujenieks wanted to prove to himself as much as to others that only his flesh, not his spirit, could be imprisoned. Along with the famous Russian dissidents Andrei Sinavsky and Yuli Daniel, he actually happened to serve his sentence in the "best university of literature in the Soviet Union": just like Nelson Mandela in his South African prison, they organized various literary and intellectual events and courses, celebrated national holidays and did everything within their power not to give in to despair but lend some sense to a senseless period of time. A few years into Skujenieks's imprisonment, Amnesty International took up his case and the Soviet authorities offered to shorten the time he was condemned to serve, but since Skujenieks considered himself innocent, he could not accept the deal since it would mean tacitly admitting his guilt. His first book of poems, *Lirika un balsis* (Lyrics and Voices), one of the most influential books of the time, came out only eleven years after his release.

Among the most interesting phenomena in the 1970s Latvian poetry were the poetic prose books by Imants Ziedonis, *Epiphanies I* (1972) and *Epiphanies II* (1974). Ziedonis started jotting down his "epiphanies" on a trip to Bulgaria where he could feel free for the very first time: even free from the need to write against the Soviet power. These flashes of inner freedom, or revelations, were a novelty in Latvian, and also Soviet, literature. Their intellectual acuteness and sparkling imagination make them as delightful today as they were then.

In the 1970s poets who had been born in the mid- or late 1940s entered the literary scene, with Uldis Bērziņš, b. 1944, Jānis Rokpelnis, b. 1945, and Leons Briedis, b. 1949, most prominent among them. Despite the seemingly impenetrable Iron Curtain, they had already mastered the main currents of Western modernism, including surrealism, much despised by the Soviet authorities, as well as the poetic output by such towering figures as T. S. Eliot, Ezra Pound and Allen Ginsberg. These young poets broke with their predecessors with the result that they, and especially Bērziņš, had to constantly fend off attackers that claimed that their poetry was obtuse and represented an insignificant detour from the main highway of Soviet poetry. There were some critical voices who tried to come to their defence, however, seeing that particularly Uldis Bērziņš is arguably one of the most original Latvian poets. Using the type of shortcut comparisons common in advertising one might even call him a hybrid of Pound and Khlebnikov.

Here is a good place to mention an important wellspring of vitality in Latvian poetry – translations. There were two specific considerations behind the unofficial drive to translate: first, to try to bring closer the ethnic groups that found themselves in the Soviet camp without the mediation of Russian; and second, since Latvian poets had practically no opportunities to travel abroad, they did the converse, that is, they brought the world to Latvia. Under the leadership of "General" Skujenieks, they divided the world not unlike the high command of an army, deciding who learnt which languages and who translated from them. The most outstanding polyglot is, again, Uldis Bērziņš who translates from a number of Turkic languages, Hebrew (the poetic books of the Old Testament), Arabic (he has recently finished a translation of the Qur'an) and is currently working on *Cantar de Mío Cid* from medieval Spanish. The many strata of foreign cultures are seamlessly adopted into his own poetry.

The late 1980s mark the début of Guntars Godiņš, b. 1958, with his ironic poems directed at the dying empire; some of them even becoming rock lyrics, for example the poem that has the sonorous refrain: "Without your own language you are just shit". With Latvia regaining independence, however, he seems to be seeking serenity and silence in Buddhist-inspired poetry. In addition, Godiņš is the principal translator of Estonian poetry in Latvian. Another star of this generation is Amanda Aizpuriete, b. 1956, finding her unique diction in erotic love, everyday life and nature alike.

Edvīns Raups, b. 1962, found his own deeply private and intense expression with his very first book of poems. Liāna Langa, b. 1960, has published three collections of poetry as well as translations from English and Russian. In the early 1990s she spent a few years in

New York, studying philosophy and twentieth-century American literature. Her dense poetry is nevertheless very concrete. In her book *Te debesis, te ciparnīca* (Here the Sky, Here the Dial, 1997) she contrasts the inner world of an individual (sky) with the mechanics of time (dial).

As the Soviet empire collapsed, it took with it its ruling poetic form, that is the quatrain with its a-b-a-b or a-b-c-b rhyme schemes. Replacing it with an individually created free verse meant liberating the language. Literature in disguise was replaced by direct speech, drawing on lexical strata that would be unthinkable in the old days, including swear words and sex terminology. A spade could now be called a spade, despite those who were shocked and detected signs of decadence and deterioration in the new poetry. While Bērziņš claimed that for him "nothing has changed. I have always written as I please", a woman poet who had survived both the war and Stalin's era once said to me: "I am so happy that I can finally write what, and the way, I please", and showed me her long poem about her colleague, the outstanding poet Vilis Cedriņš whose boat en route to the safety of Sweden was intercepted by Soviet coastguard, and who perished in some Gulag camp.

If I were to attempt a brief summary of the history of Latvian poetry, it would look like this: in the mid-nineteenth century, Latvian poetry – along with recognition and celebration of the nation's past – evolved as a part of the larger project of finding a distinct identity. By the early twentieth century, there were already different kinds of poetry – from politically radical to symbolist (decadent). The First World War was followed by modernism, futurism, imagism. The non-violent *coup d'état* of Kārlis Ulmanis opened the door to a kind of nationalist parochialism, yet it should be borne in mind that left-leaning poets were still allowed to publish. The early postwar period was marked by Stalinism, which damaged Latvian poetry by expecting it to produce paeans to "the world's greatest genius", the communist party and "the Motherland of the proletariat". In Sweden and the United States, however, young poets continued to develop modernism. In Latvia, poetry recovered after the death of Stalin and the Twentieth Party Congress in 1956. There were communist authors who demanded that writers be allowed to depict the shady side of life along with the sunny one (O. Vācietis). The 1960s were marked by liberation from socialist realism, political protest and defence of the Latvian people and language expressed between lines: the poet was looked upon as the nation's voice. The 1970s brought about more introspection, a more varied poetic language and innovations of form that became less accessible to the general public. The 1980s revealed how weak the Empire's hold was on people's minds: young poets published overtly ironic poetry of the kind that would have been unthinkable before; the national awakening at the end of the decade brought to the foreground patriotic poetry produced for the moment. The first post-Soviet years and beyond were characterized by individualism both in form and content. It is impossible to detect particular currents or trends. Nor is poetry the nation's rostrum any longer: in terms of popularity it is losing to the hitherto living nerve as expressed by poets in their thirties – is a match to the poetry written by their peers in the West.

I hope to have at least sketched in two important matters: why one should not be interested in Latvian poetry and why one should. While I have been working on this introduction in the sunny Latvian port city of Ventspils, I have been meeting beautiful women, tourists from all over the world, and NATO soldiers – on the streets and on the beach, in parks with big old trees and on the waterfront with its huge ships and private yachts. I would call it the summer manoeuvres: stimulating with its idyll and drama, just like poetry.

Juris Kronbergs
Ventspils, 2010

ANNA AUZIŅA

PHOTO: MĀRTIŅŠ ZĀLĪTIS

Anna Auziņa was born in 1975 in Riga. Growing up in a family of writers, she began publishing her poetry as early as 1990. Auziņa studied Fine Arts and has been exhibiting her paintings since 1994. Having spent five reluctant years in advertising, she has, so far, published two prize-winning volumes of poetry – *Atšķirtie dārzi* (Opened Gardens / Riga: Uguns, 1995) and *Slēpotāji bučojas sniegā* (Skiers Kissing in the Snow / Riga: Preses nams, 2001) – with her third, *Es izskatījos laimīga* (I Looked Happy / Riga: Mansards, 2010), short-listed for the Annual Literature Prize. The poems in this anthology have been drawn from all three.

BROKASTIS MĀKOŅOS

reizēm ir tik labi
ka varētu vēl kādus bērnus
suņus kaķus kāmjus
zivtiņas pustrakas vecvecmammas
divas trīs teltis
slēpes datoru
vairākus monitorus
salādētu to visu un ņemtu līdzi

brokastis zaļumos
varbūt labāk mākoņos
jānopērk piknika piederumi

un labi āķi
lai trose bez bažām
mūs debesīs uzvelk
mēs mākoņos desiņas cepsim
kā vienmēr
un vēlāk tu mani pliku
debesīs pafilmēsi

kad mākoņos aizmiguši
būs bērni
suņi kaķi kāmji
zivtiņas pustrakās vecvecmammas

* * *

es jums panākšu pretī līdz vārtiņiem
tālāk nedrīkst

iepazīsimies tā esmu es
maziņa slikta
šeit man ir vasarnīca

iepazīsimies dārzs ir zaļš
bet tik ļoti gribas aiz vārtiņiem

kur tie laimīgie brīvie bērni
spēlē badmintonu
uz brauktuves

BREAKFAST IN THE CLOUDS

sometimes it feels so good
that we could have more children
dogs cats hamsters
tropical fish batty great grandmas
two or three tents
skis a computer
several monitors
just load it all up and take along

breakfast on the grass
better yet in the clouds
have to buy picnic gear

and good hooks
so that the rope can hoist us up
to the sky safely
in the clouds we'll cook sausages
as we normally do
and then you'll take pictures
of me in the sky naked

when they have all fallen asleep in the clouds
children
dogs cats hamsters
tropical fish batty great grandmas

* * *

to meet you I will come up to the gate
I'm not allowed beyond

let's get acquainted it's me
little bad me
this is our summer house

let's get acquainted the garden is green
but I so want to go past the gate

where the happy free children
play badminton
out on the street

* * *

es vēlētos viena pati
dzīvot mājā vecā un lielā
visapkārt lai nav neviena
tikai daudz lietu
un es aizbāztu šķirbas ar vati
un lai ciemiņi retumis nāktu pa vienam
durvis stāvētu vaļā
viss būtu aizmidzis pamests
tik vecs jauks un izlietots
vējš saule nāktu pie manis pa logiem
varbūt man varētu būt
kāds bēbis vai dzīvnieks ko kopt
un es līdzīgi kukaiņiem lidoņiem šaudītos
pa māju veco un lielo
kurai līdzīgu es savu dvēseli vēlētos
un lai ciemiņi retumis nāktu pa vienam

* * *

ir tādas laimīgu cilvēku ielas
uzkāp un esi laimīgs

(varam ņemt kādu gājēju ielu pie jūras,
taču Elizejas lauku platās ietves arī ļoti labi der;
un lai ir saulains, ne pārāk karsti, bet drīkst būt arī tumsa ar lampiņām;
un tad lai tur piemīlīgi cilvēki pastaigājas, lai kafejnīcu daudz, lai mūzika,
vienmēr svētdiena vai vismaz vasaras vakars;
un tu ej pa šo ielu un pretī visi nāk priecīgi, tikai jāizvēlas, kurš krodziņš
jaukāks, kurš saldējums gardāks)

laimīgas ielas kā slīdošās lentes
uzkāp un esi laimīgs
nokāp un vairs neesi laimīgs

* * *

I would like to be alone
living in a house ancient and large
so that no one is around
only plenty of things
and I would stuff cotton into the cracks
and each guest would come single
the door would stay open
everything would be dozing abandoned
so old pleasant and worn
sun wind would come to me through the windows
perhaps I might have
a baby or a pet to look after
and just like a flying insect I'd buzz
through the house ancient and large
which I'd wish my soul would be like
and for guests to come seldom and single

* * *

there are these streets of happy people
step on them and be happy

(for instance, some pedestrian street by the sea,
but the wide pavements of Champs Elysées will do just as well;
and it should be sunny, not too hot, or it could be dark, with street lights;
and nice people should be strolling there, many cafés should be there as well, and music and an ongoing Sunday or a summer night at least;
and you go down such street and everyone you meet is happy, all you have to do is decide which bar is nicer, which ice-cream more delicious)

happy streets are like conveyor belts
step on and you're happy
step off and happy you're not

* * *

Ir vēl kas.
Man kādas sievietes briesmīgi pietrūkst.
Viņa pavada lidmašīnas.
Viņa reizēm smaržo pēc ledus, pēc mežcirtēja un darvas,
bet citkārt pēc siltas melones daivas.
Viņa klusē kā ezers un elpo kā sala naktī.
Viņa apsnieg kā rītausmā slidotava.
Es gribētu viņu šurpu, lai apguļas smiltīs.
Ar kaulu un ar kristālu es buru,
bet es nezinu vairs, vai pa kvēlošām krāsmatām auļo viņas zirgs,
vai dus viņa tīmekļos rasotā pļavā.

* * *

Izvēle pacēlās spārnos,
mīkstām pārslām nolaidās atteikšanās.
Miegs apskāvieni žalūzijas ilūzijas.
Mēness aptieka vaļā, saules aptieka ciet.
Kad rīts un pavasaris atkal pienāks?

Mīlēt kādu un ļaut viņam iet.
Un atpakaļ nākt, un iet, un atpakaļ nākt, un iet.

Bet dzīve. Siers vīns alga viesības,
lietus putekšņi laime izvēle sviestmaize negaiss,
draudzenes runājas, viņš atlidojis ar visu to kazu,
pavasaris tomēr atnāk. Un maijs, maijs pāri malai.
Bērni atgriezušies no laukiem klaigā.
Dzīve varbūt vajadzētu vēl.

Pārbraucam naktī tu pasmejies.
Aizmugurējā sēdeklī mazas lūpas
jau dziesmai līdzi māk kustēties.

Es mīlu es mīlu es gribu ļaut iet.
Kad saules aptieka vaļā, jau mēness aptieka ciet.

* * *

And something else.
I terribly miss one woman.
She sees aeroplanes off.
Sometimes she smells of ice, lumberjacks and tar
but sometimes of a warm slice of melon.
She is silent like a lake and breathes like an island at night.
Snow settles on her like on a skating-rink at dawn.
I would like to get her over here to lie down in the sand.
I try to conjure her with bones and with crystal,
but if her horse gallops over smouldering ruins
or she slumbers amongst cobwebs in dew-covered grass
I no longer know.

* * *

Choice took wing
renunciation descended in soft flakes.
Sleep embrace jalousie illusion
The moon pharmacy open, sun pharmacy closed.
When will the morning when will spring come?

To love someone and let him go.
And come back and go and come back and go.

But life. Cheese wine salary party,
rain pollen happiness choice sandwich thunder
girlfriends talk, he flew back with that cow,
spring arrives after all. And May, May is running over.
Children back from the country are shouting.
Life perhaps should have more.

We are driving back in the middle of the night you laugh.
In the back seat tiny lips
already know how to follow a song.

I love I love I want to let go.
When sun pharmacy's open, the moon pharmacy's closed.

* * *

Jau vairākus gadus tu nelaupi manu mieru, tu esi man paklausījis. Tu nezini to rītu, tu nezini balto kreklu, tu nezini ziemas sauli, tu nezini vēstules lasītāju. Jo dzīvot, dzīvot es gribu. Es reizumis atminu dziesmas, visskaistākās, plosītājas, es tām nedrīkstu ļauties. Un es likšu vannā savu mīļuci mazo, savu pīkstuli, savu kakuci. Es gribēju gaismas, es gribēju jūras, tavas sirdis mirgoja visur, kamēr aiztecēja. Bet teic, vai gan tev būtu vieglāk, ja tu zinātu, kāpēc. Mēs varētu aizbraukt pie Volgas, uz Samāru, Kostromu aizbraukt. Un aizvērt acis. Un iegulties zālē. Mēs varētu aizbraukt pat abi. Ir tas nekā nemainītu. Taču reiz pienāks diena, kad baismi skaistajām balsīm es ļaušos. Un lai paņem mani virpuļi melnie un sirdis lai visas manas salūtā debesīs izplaukst un nobirst pār zemi. Un kāda varbūt tev plaukstās. Jo dzīvot, dzīvot es gribu.

* * *

Kad es, naktī pārnākusi,
pieeju viņai sakārtot segu,
reizēm viņa klusējot
maigi glāsta man seju.

Viņa nesaka, ka es smirdu,
un neprasa, kur es biju,
tikai glāsta manu seju
maziem pirkstiņiem.

* * *

ko tu dari
kad tu esi mikēniete
virs pavarda tava nav jumta
tur ielīst lietus
kļūst tavs pavards kā baseins?
vai tu mazgā tur matus
peldini savus bērnus
un kā dūņās to kājas grimst pelnos?
lieti šeit laikam ir silti

* * *

For several years already you've left me in peace, you have listened. You don't know that morning, you don't know the white shirt, don't know the winter sun, don't know the letter reader. For I want to live, to live I want. Sometimes I remember songs, the most beautiful ones, the ones that tear one apart, I cannot give in to them. And I will bathe my little darling my little screamer my little pooper. I wanted light, I wanted the sea, your hearts were glowing everywhere until they ran out. But tell me would it be easier for you if you knew why. We could go to the Volga, to Samara, to Kostroma. And close our eyes. And lie down on the grass. We could even go just the two of us. Even that would change nothing. Yet the day will come when I give in to the terrifying beautiful voices. And let the black whirlwinds take me and let all my hearts bloom in heavenly fireworks and scatter all over the earth. And one perhaps will fall in your hands. For I want to live, to live I want.

* * *

When home late at night
I go to tuck her in,
sometimes, without a word,
she gently caresses my face.

She doesn't say that I stink,
she does not ask where I've been,
just caresses my face
with those tiny fingers of hers.

* * *

what do you do
when you are a Mycenaean
there is no roof over your hearth
rain pours in
your hearth turns into a pool?
do you wash your hair there
bathe your children
so their feet stick in the ash as in sludge?
rains must be warm here

bet ko gan jūs tad ēdat
vai iebriduši pavardā
tu un tavs mīļais vien krītošās debesis dzerat?
saki – kad tu esi mikēniete
ko dari kad pavardā tavā līst lietus?

* * *

Man tagad ir sunītis,
viņu sauc Nemiers, no rūgtās sugas (vēlāk būs bildīte arī).
Viņš brauc man azotē līdzi uz darbu,
viņš diemžēl seko man bērnistabā un vakaros prasās ārā.
Viņam nepietiek druscin tepat pie durvīm, viņam vajag vējā un lietū.
Es zinu, tu uztraucies, bet mēs jau tikai pa apgaismotajām ielām,
un tik ilgi vien tālab, lai kārtīgi piekūst – tā mums visiem būs labāk.
Lai negaudo vēlāk pie guļamistabas durvīm, kuras tu rūpīgi aizver
viņam deguna priekšā.

* * *

Mana sieviete ar ugunskura matiem
Andrē Bretons

Mans vīrietis ar jūras acīm rietā
Ar vižņu acīm
Aiz dūmakas plakstiņiem
Ar neona skatieniem
Mans vīrietis vienu aci piemiedzis
Mans vīrietis ar leduslāča dvēseli
Viņa krastos ir aļģes
Viņa fjordos grūti izkuģot
Mans vīrietis
kura piere ir aisbergs
Gar kura pieri peld mākoņi
Kura pierē plaukst sniegpulksteņi
Mans vīrietis ar pusdienlaika matiem
Ar matiem pūpolvītoliem
Ar matiem kas atritinās kā zīda baķis
Kura vaigi ir pļauti lauki
Kur čūskas lodā
Un braukā traktoriņi

but what do you eat then
or do you and your lover wade into the hearth
to drink from the falling sky?
tell me, when you are a Mycenaean,
what do you do when it rains in your hearth?

* * *

I now have a doggie
his name is Disquiet, he's of the bitter breed (later will post a picture)
He comes with me to work tucked under my arm
sadly, he follows me to the nursery and in the evening wants out.
Right here by the door just won't do, he has to go out in the rain and wind.
I know you worry but we stay on the well-lit streets,
and only until he gets really tired, it's best that way for everyone
So that he doesn't howl by the bedroom door which you carefully shut
right in his face.

* * *

Ma Femme à la chevelure de feu de bois
André Breton

My man with eyes of sea at sunset
With ice floe eyes
Behind eyelids of mist
With neon glances
My man squinting with one eye
My man with a polar bear's soul
Seaweed on his shores
Difficult to sail through his fjords
My man
whose forehead is an iceberg
Along whose forehead clouds float
On whose forehead snowdrops bloom
My man with hair of noon
With pussy-willow hair
With hair that unfolds like a piece of silk
Whose cheeks are mown fields
With snakes crawling
And tractors chugging

Mans vīrietis
kura kakls ir negaiss
Un kura deguns ir tvaikonītis
Kura vēders kūp kā pavasara augsne
Mans vīrietis
Kura krūtis ir stikla kalni
Kura krūtis ir raudu mūris
Kura pleci ir senmeža koku saknes
Un pils pakāpieni
Mans vīrietis ar Islandes ķērpjiem padusēs
Viņa lāpstiņas ir klintis
Viņa viduklis ir stirna
Un pirmais sniegs
Viņa mugura ir slēpošanas trase
Viņa dibens ir futbolbumba un vakardienas bulciņas
Viņa kājas ir ūdenstorņi
Viņa rokas ir kaijas un ligzda vienlaikus
Viņa pēdas ir līdakas
Un viņa delnas ir laši
Viņa delnās deg kūla
Viņa pirksti ir ultraīsviļņi
Un niedru stabulītes
Viņa nagi ir ledenes
Un veci gliemežvāki
Mans vīrietis
Kura cirkšņi ir laipas
Kura klēpī ir grantsbedres
Kura daikts ir lāsteka
Kura pauti ir jūras oļi
Un zaļi tomātiņi
Mans vīrietis
kura bērni piedzimstot smaržoja tik mīļi
Kuram pašam ir zīdaiņa mute
Troļļa mute pie krūtsgala
Klusēšanas zvēresta mute
Kapenes ausis
Mans vīrietis elpu aizturējis
Mans vīrietis novērsies
Mans vīrietis dzelme dārzs un aizvējš
Mans vīrietis ceļos nometies
Bijībā

My man
whose neck is a thunderstorm
And whose nose is a steamboat
Whose belly steams like soil in spring
My man
Whose chest is a mountain of glass
Whose chest is the wailing wall
Whose shoulders are roots of an ancient forest
And castle steps
My man with Icelandic moss in his armpits
His shoulder blades are cliffs
His waist is a deer
And the first snow
His back is a ski run
His ass is a football and yesterday's rolls
His legs are water towers
His arms are both seagulls and their nest
His feet are pike
His hands are salmon
Last year's grass burns in his hands
His fingers are ultra-shortwave
And reed flutes
His nails are bonbons
And old seashells
My man
Whose groins are bridges
Whose lap has gravel pits
Whose dick is an icicle
Whose balls are sea pebbles
And green tomatoes
My man
whose children being born smelled so sweet
Who himself has a baby's mouth
Troll's mouth at a nipple
Mouth of an oath of silence
Ears of a vault
My man holding his breath
My man turned away
My man the deep the garden the shelter
My man on his knees
In awe

MŪSU MĀTES

mūsu abu mātes – viņas ir laupītājvecenes
ceļa malā sēž plati ieplestām kājām
un pīpē pīpi

mūsu mātes ir arī lauku sievas
apēd sulīgu ābolu un aiziet pļaut govij zāli

mūsu mātes ir raganas
tumšās virtuvēs kurina plītis gluži kā ellē
un kaut ko vāra

un viņas ir arī baigās hetēras
tādas melnas krāsotām acīm
un vīnainām lūpām

un vēl mūsu mātes ir vājprātīgās
garos baltos kreklos
milzīgām acīm
bez zobiem
un krata kaulainos pirkstus

un vēl mūsu mātes ir bērni
slapjām cirtām pār apaļiem vaigiem
kad viņas izraudājušās beidzot aizmieg

* * *

Naktī mēs braucām
uz Sauku, uz ezeru. Tumšas un grūtas ir tava brāļa acis,
varbūt mēs pelnījuši
šīs sūrmes krūkas pilnās un šīs milzīgo suņu acis pieplūdušās
mūžam līdzi?

Mani mīļie, dzeja nemaz nav tā, kas jums liekas. Tā ir vilnis, filma, miljons sīku radību, elpu cērt ciet, un prātā pulsējoši viedi vārdi. Kā reizēm tā izlien no miglas, mozaīkas tad maigas, kaķa ķepiņu pelēksārtas, kā saule rāmi no dūmakas izpeld, silti ceļi un silti ceļgali peļķēs.

OUR MOTHERS

both our mothers – they are robber molls
sitting by the side of the road with legs spread wide
and smoking pipes

our mothers are also country women
they eat juicy apples and go to mow grass for the cow

our mothers are witches
stoking fires in dark kitchens just like in hell
stirring some brew

and they are also quite some hetairas
black with painted eyes
with wine stained lips

and our mothers are madwomen
in long white jackets
with huge eyes
without any teeth
wagging their bony fingers

and our mothers are children
with damp curls over round cheeks
when after a good cry they finally doze off

* * *

In the middle of the night we went
to Sauka, to the lake. Dark and heavy are your brother's eyes,
perhaps we deserve
these overflowing flasks and these brimming eyes of huge dogs
always along?

Poetry, my dears, is not at all what you think. It is a wave, a film, millions of tiny creatures choking you up and wise words pulsing in the brain. How it sometimes crawls out of the fog, mosaics are gentle then, rosy gray like cat's paws, how the sun quietly comes out of the mist, warm roads and warm knees in the puddles.

Bet te tā asiem kliedzieniem
un pretstatos savos virzībā,
mežonīgā ātrumā mēs braucām uz Sauku,
nežēlīgi ritmi un negaisi, gaisma svītrās, propelleri un čuksti karsti, un mātes aizmirst, cik viņām gadu, laimīga ir viņu zeme, kur ap ezeriem birzīs takas un dziesmas jūdzēm tālu.

Taču ziniet, es reiz mīlēju kādu dzejnieku,
pēcāk nekad vairs nespēju atmest esmi savu,
ne aizmirst, ne atdot.

Mēs braucām uz Sauku,
katrs ar savu sāpi ļāvāmies ceļam un satikām zilbaltu pūci,
miers lai ir ar zemessargiem Susējas pagriezienā un pāri
tukšajiem laukumiem nakts,
nekādu pamestību tie nepauž, šie vispiepildītākie,
kuros nejēdzīgā skaistumā dzeja skaidra strāvo
vai staro tavas acis
visgaišākās.
Un varbūt es palikšu tajās.

* * *

Negribu tevi tai visā iesaistīt, negribu nogruzīt, negribu vārdā saukt. Forši jau tie citroni būtu, un arī ziedi laikam ir skaisti, ja vien sagaida piektās paaudzes zaru. Uzpotēt vieglāk. Mute ciet, taču iznāk pa nāsīm tavs vārds. Bedrītē iešņākts citrona podā. Nu visi smiesies un dusmosies, nomētās, iemīs. Eju un gaidu. Neviens neko. Šajās mājās ūdens diemžēl ir kaļķains, citronam nepatīk. Filtrēju, nelīdz. Stāvam atkal ar tevi uz stūra un kaut ko jau es lasu tev acīs. Es to citrona sēklu iestādīju vēl jauna kad biju, vēl vecajās mājās, un toreiz auga it sulīgs. Bet šeit man tas kaļķainais ūdens. Būs laikam jāatdod kādam citam, varbūt sagaidīs piektās paaudzes zaru vai uzpotēs ko nebūt virsū un ziedi tad plauks. Un citroni briedīs un šķīdīs un pušumos kodīs tavs vārds.

Whereas here shouting sharply
directed by its contradictions,
we speeded wildly to Sauka,
merciless rhythms and thunderstorms, light in streaks, propellers and hot whispers, and mothers forget their years, happy their land, with paths in groves around lakes and songs heard from miles afar.

Yet you must know, I once loved a poet
and later could never give up my being,
could not forget, could not give back.

We drove to Sauka,
each with their own pain we yielded to the road and met a blue-white owl, peace be with the home-guard at the exit to Susēja and over
vacant lots there's night,
there is no abandonment in the most fulfilled ones,
in whom poetry flows clear,
or your eyes radiate
at their brightest.
And in them I just may remain.

* * *

I do not want to involve you, do not want to burden you, do not want to call your name. Lemons would naturally be cool and the flowers I guess are beautiful if only you wait for a fifth generation branch. Easier to graft. My mouth is closed yet your name passes through the nostrils. Hissed in a hole in the lemon pot soil. Everyone will laugh now and get angry and stone me and trample me. I go and I wait. Nothing happens. At this house the water has too much lime, the lemon-tree does not like it. Filtering did not help. We are standing on the corner again and your eyes are already telling me something. I planted that lemon seed when I was still young, still in the old house, and then it was even quite lush. But here that limy water. I guess I'll have to give it away, perhaps they will wait for the fifth generation or engraft it with something and then it will bloom. And lemons will grow and burst open and your name will sting in the sores.

* * *

pienāk rudens
varavīksni grib glāzē man liet
šķiet nekas nav pie sirds ķēries
patīk man saulainā parkā
kamēr mana meitiņa dzied
lasīt grāmatu
kuru aizņēmos
vēl pavasarī no tevis

viss ir labi un jauki
mans laiks
varavīksnē kāpj mutē smeļas
patīk man parkā lasīt
kamēr meitiņa dzied
tomēr kaut kā man šoruden sāp tava seja

tavi pianista pirksti man sūrst
tavi riņķi zem acīm tumst man
tavs zoda izliekums gaist
visos parka kokos tu drebi
visās lapās man atveries

viņa nāks un mēs iesim strūklaku skatīties
pasmaidīšu un aizvēršu ciet
grāmatu
kuru vēl pavasarī no tevis

patīk man parkā lasīt
kamēr meitiņa dzied

TOMĒR KAUT KAS NAV KĀRTĪBĀ

Atvasaras svētdiena silta
Viņi piestātnē blakus stāv
Promenāde un zivju tirgus
Tomēr kaut kas nav kārtībā

Lapas līgani krīt no kokiem
Krāsaini baloni paceļas
Ļaudis visapkārt smaida un čalo
Tomēr kaut kas nav kārtībā

* * *

autumn comes
ready to pour rainbow into my glass
seems nothing I've taken close to heart
I like to sit in a sunlit park
while my daughter is singing
and read a book
I borrowed
just this spring from you

everything is fine and dandy
my time
climbs rainbows gets in my mouth
I like to read in the park
while my daughter is singing
only I find that your face hurts me this season

your pianist's fingers are smarting
circles under your eyes are darkening under mine
the angle of your chin is vanishing
in all the trees you are trembling
in all my pages opening

she will come and we'll go to look at the fountain
I will smile and close
the book
which from you just this spring

I like to read in the park
while my daughter is singing

YET SOMETHING SEEMS WRONG

A warm Sunday in autumn
They stand together at a stop
Promenade and fish market
Yet something seems wrong

Leaves gently fly off from the trees
Coloured balloons rise upward
People all around are smiling and talking
Yet something seems wrong

Viņš ir stiprs pleci ir plati
Krekls labi tam izskatās
Viņa ir daiļa un laikam grūta
Tomēr kaut kas nav kārtībā

Varbūt nelaime balonu pušķī
Varbūt zem baznīcas kupola
Varbūt vienam no viņiem ir smagi
Kas gan ar viņiem nav kārtībā

Varbūt viņai vēders par šķību
Viņam cepure neturas
Varbūt laipa ir sliktā leņķī
Kaut kas tai visā nav kārtībā

Pavisam maigi šūpojas laipa
Rokas vieglītēm saskaras
Es viņus radīju
Bet es nezinu
Kas ar viņiem nav kārtībā

* * *

Tu izskatījies laimīgs
Kā pieneņpūka sirds

Es izskatījos laimīga
Kliedēta gaisma pār pļavu

Vai varam būt draugi
Vasarsvētku ņirba

Kukaiņi tekalē, bērni skraida, un nesāp, nesāp it nemaz. Mēs vēl sēdēsim uz terases, mēs vēl malkosim vīnu, mēs šūposimies šūpolēs, pēc svina apvāršņiem, strauti burbuļos, pasaules noglāstīs viena otru. Ripos ķegļu bumbas, putni aiztrauksies, laivinieki piestās krastā.

Kur palikuši, kur palikuši visi garie gadi.

Tu izskatījies laimīgs
Saule lēnām riet

He is strong broad-shouldered
His shirt fits him so well
She is pretty and seems to be pregnant
Yet something seems wrong

Perhaps the problem is in the balloons
Perhaps under the church's dome
Perhaps one of them is grieving
What could be wrong with them

Is her belly perhaps distended
Is his hat not sitting right
Is the foot bridge at a wrong angle
Something in all that seems wrong

The footbridge is swaying quite gently
Their hands touch ever so lightly
I'm their creator
Yet I am not sure
What is wrong with these two

* * *

You looked happy
Heart like dandelion fluff

I looked happy
Mellow light over the field

Can we be friends
Whitsuntide ripples

Insects crawling about, kids running, and there is no pain, no pain at all. We will still sit on the terrace, we will sip wine, we will swing on the swings, after the leaden horizons, brooks will bubble, worlds will caress each other. Skittle balls will roll, birds will dash away, boaters will come ashore.

Where, where have all these years gone.

You looked happy
The sun slowly setting

Es izskatījos laimīga
Mazliet pierimst vējš

Vai varam būt draugi
Migla klusu kāpj

Tu izskatījies laimīgs

* * *

varu uzzīmēt beigto strazdu
atkal zarā sēžam
pirmo mīlēto suni atkal skrienam
rozā istabu bērnības ielā
varu zīmēt ko vien es gribu

varu uzzīmēt tēti jaunu
varu uzzīmēt vecmammu dzīvu
zīmēt veselus tos kas slimi
es varu zīmēt visu ko
it neviens man to nevar aizliegt

varu eņģeļus varu velnus
varu zīmēt visus ko mīlu
arī pat tos kas prom no manis
kā arī tos kas mani nemīl
un viņi man nevarēs pretoties

VĒL ILGI PIRMS

Ar jaunības tamboradatu es tavu kamzoli pielaboju. Tas saplosīts vējā, še, kur mēs tagad mītam. Kaut kur ābeļzari pār upi tik smagi liecas un mājas ir ar galiem pret ielām. Kad rudens būs galā, man būs jādzemdē bērns.

Es noķēru līgavas pušķi. Pār Vitebskas jokainām mājām es lidoju tavās skavās un še nu mēs atkal esam. Kāpj migla no rīta, un dārzos plaukst dālijas treknas. Tās nosals un āboli nobirs. Un tad būs jādzemdē bērns.

I looked happy
The wind dying down

Can we be friends
Fog quietly rising

You looked so happy

* * *

I can draw the dead thrush
perched on a branch once again
the first dog I loved running
the pink room on my childhood street
I can draw what I want

I can draw daddy young
I can draw grandma alive
I can draw healthy those who are sick
I can draw anything
and no one at all can stop me

I can draw angels I can draw devils
I can draw all whom I love
and even those who are away
and those who do not love me
they won't be able to argue

LONG BEFORE

With the crochet hook of youth I mended your sweater. It was torn by the wind here where we live now. Somewhere apple branches lean over the river heavy and houses stand ends to the street. When the fall is over I will have to give birth.

I caught the bridal bouquet. Over the strange houses of Vitebsk I flew in your embrace and here we are once again. Fog rises in mornings and ample dahlias bloom in the gardens. They will get frostbitten and apples will fall. And then I will have to give birth.

Būs vēlāk tie paši valši un garie galdi tie paši. Un nodzeltējušie lauki. Un mājas ar galiem pret ielām. Ēd līgava biešu zupu un vēlāk tā raksta – nav arī rudenī miera un visam pāri milzīgās skumjas. Un kad skumjas būs galā, man būs jādzemdē bērns.

* * *

When I was a Hershey bar – in my father's back pocket
Laurie Anderson

Kā lai esmu tavs eņģelis, kukulīt.
Es neredzu, neredzu ceļu savu gaišo, laikam klapes uz acīm un aizbāžņi ausīs manās. Kā lai esmu tavs eņģelis, ja domas man sniegā, ja Salavecis nejauki prasa – vai šogad biji laba māte? Bet tu guli, mana saulīte, mana pelīte, mana bitīte.

Mēs vispār diezgan normāli vecāki esam, sapulces apmeklējam, nadziņi nogriezti, drēbītes tīras, kastaņus salasām un tukšas piena pakas laicīgi iedodam līdzi, zina adresi nosaukt, zina savu dzimšanas dienu, katru gadu braucam salūtu skatīties, braucam kartupeļus rakt.

Ma-ni na-mi. Ma-ni li-ni. Mam-ma mīl ma-ni.
Kalcija netrūkst un dzelzs.

Tikai laiks tevi šķir no mammas sarkanā mēteļa atvēruma, no pusizkusušās šokolādītes tēva džinsu kabatā. Tikai laiks tevi šķir no Salaveča jautājumiem un no tā, ko es ieraugu sniegā. Murmulīti manu, runkulīti.

Mani lini. Mani nami. Laiks ir vienmēr pret mani.

Later there will be the same waltzes and the same long tables. And the rust coloured fields. And houses ends facing the street. The bride eats beet soup and later she writes: no peace in autumn and this great sadness over everything. And when the sadness is over I will have to give birth.

* * *

When I was a Hershey bar – in my father's back pocket

Laurie Anderson

How can I be your angel, honeybun.
I can't, I can't see my path ever so bright, I must have blinders on and earplugs in. How can I be your angel if my thoughts are under the snow and Father Frost questions me sternly: were you a good mother this year? But you go to sleep, my sunshine, my kitten, my little chickadee.

We are in fact quite normal parents, we go to meetings, fingernails are cut, clothes are clean, we pick horse chestnuts and provide milk cartons to take along on time, address has been memorized, so has the birthday, every year we go to watch fireworks and to harvest potatoes.

Ma-ni na-mi. Ma-ni li-ni. Mam-ma mīl ma-ni.
No calcium lacking or iron.

Only time separates you from the slit in your mum's red coat, from the melted chocolate in dad's jeans pocket. Only time separates you from Father Frost's questions and from what I see in the snow. My little pumpkin, my lambkin.

Mani lini. Mani nami. Time is always against me.

Note: The italicized text is quoted from a Latvian ABC teaching children to put syllables together: "My houses. My flax. Mum loves me."

INGMĀRA BALODE

PHOTO: AUTHOR'S ARCHIVE

INGMĀRA BALODE was born in 1981 in Auce and is a poet and translator currently working for *¼ Satori* Culture and Philosophy Website. Having studied sculpture and applied arts in college, she also has experience in culture management. She has been publishing her poetry since 1997, and received the Prize for the Best Debut in Latvian Literature for her first collection *Ledenes, ar kurām var sagriezt mēli* (Bonbons That May Cut Your Tongue / Riga: ¼ Satori) in 2007. As a translator, Balode is mostly interested in twentieth- and twenty-first century Polish and American poets (e.e. cummings, Adam Zagayewski, J. Schuyler *et al*). The poems that follow include some from a yet-to-be-published volume of poetry.

AIZVĒRTS

neatrauju no tevis tumsā acis
lai arī tumsa kā pēdējais soģis un kungs
ir norāvusi man tevi tev pasauli pasaulei pasaules zaļgano ādu
aptinusi ceļus un vadus ar mākoņu šķedelēm

tā ir nāve neatliek nekas cits kā to atklāt

viss tiek klusumā pārvērsts
tāda vieta

neatrauju no tevis tumsā acis

ATVĒRTS

tevī ir atvērts kaut kas ko aizvērt nevar tāpat kā
nevari puķei piespiest aizvērties tāpat kā
iet kaķis tu nevari viņu apturēt nevari zināt

tevī ir atvērta pēdējā vasaras nakts
tai pāri lec zvaigznes kā tādas kas zina
kas gaidāms un sievietes dzeltenās kleitās
pieplok debesīm spiežas kā pēdas pret pēdām
pēdējā uzticības kailumā

ne tu to vari norakstīt ne noplēst ne aizdziedāt prom
pārlūst tas milzums un tomēr ne pilīte nenopil
zemē
kā zelts kā smiltis mēs esam un izbirstam paši sev cauri
mēs lieli kā milži kā pilis
neredzami tumši kā ozolā
noslēpies putns

un trausli bet tomēr mums iekšā
tik daudz dzīves kas atdzimst
kā lapeglei
sīki
gaišdzelteni stari

CLOSED

i don't take my eyes off you in the dark
though the dark as the final judge and master
has pulled you off me the world off you the green world skin off the world
wrapped knees and cables in tatters of clouds

it is death there's nothing else to do but to reveal that

everything transformed in silence
that kind of place

i don't take my eyes off you in the dark

OPEN

there is something open in you same as
you cannot force a flower to close same as
a cat walks you cannot stop him you cannot know

the last night of summer is open in you
stars leap over it as ones that know
what to expect and women in yellow dresses
press to the sky press as feet against feet
in the last nakedness of trust

you can neither write nor tear nor sing it off
all that vastness breaks up yet no drop drips to the
ground
like gold like sand we are and flow through ourselves
we are huge like giants like castles
invisible dark like a bird
hiding in an oak tree

and fragile too yet inside us
there is so much life that is reborn
like tiny
light yellow rays on a
larch

* * *

es biju uzzīmēta nodilumā alumīnija karotes liekumā es biju krūzītē kam mazliet nodauzīta krāsa es biju citronu koka lielajā cietajā lapā ar brūniem robiņiem

es biju tajā vietā kur no margām nozāģēta atslēga

veca pulksteņa uzvelkamajā atsperē mājoju
un čella kājā kas translēja bahu caur grīdu

kaimiņu bērns pie dilušiem krāsns podiņiem spoguļojās

es biju starp pirkstiem kad paberzē citrona lapu un saka – rau smaržo kā īstā āfrikā

biju metāla krāsas skabargainā plēksnē kas pieskārās visu aizmirsušai vēsai delnai

biju starp lūpām kad dzēra izklaidīgi dilstošu sulu no krūzes
un es biju bahs kas pa biezajām sijām un sienām pagrabā nokāpj

un iesūcas akmens grīdā vietumis spīdīgā

zem kuras dilst upe

LABVAKAR, GOGĒNA KUNGS.

Paul Gauguin *Bonjour, Monsieur Gauguin.*
1889. Národni Galerie, Praha

(pirmā)

Es izvēlos visus veidus kā vienlaikus dzīvot un mirt
piedzimu, pavēru muti, un, palūk, uzradās drosme [pateikt šos vārdus, ko citi raksta līdz sirmumam dziļi, bet man] – neldzīgā drosme
vienlaikus prom iet un nākt, vienlaikus sasveicināties un atvadīties.
Labvakar, Gogēna kungs, neaizskariet mani.
Neaizskariet mani, mana miesa ir izdāļāta
vakarēdienos un brokastīs, aizvesta ar kuģiem un lidmašīnām.

* * *

i was drawn in the worn out spot in the aluminium bend of the spoon
i was in the cup with the chipped paint i was in the big taut leaf of the lemon tree the leaf with the tiny brown notches

i was in that spot where a padlock has been sawn off the railing

i dwelt in the wind-up spring of an old clock
in the spike of a cello broadcasting bach through the floorboards

a neighbour's child admiring her reflection in the worn tiles of a stove

i was between the fingers as a lemon leaf is rubbed between them with the words, see, smells like real africa

i was in the splintery shard of painted metal touching a palm cool and forgetful

i was between the two lips as they absently sipped juice wearing it down in the pitcher
and i was bach descending down the thick wood beams and walls into the basement

seeping into the stone floor shiny in places

with the river waning below

GOOD EVENING, MR. GAUGUIN

Paul Gauguin *Bonjour, Monsieur Gauguin*
1889. Národni Galerie, Praha

(first)

I choose all methods for living at the same time as dying
I was born, opened my mouth and lo' I had courage [to say these words that some write till they are long in the tooth, but I have] this mad courage
to leave at the same time as coming back,
to tip my hat in greeting at the same time as taking my leave.
Good evening, Mr. Gauguin, do not touch me.
Do not touch me, my flesh has been dished out
at last suppers and breakfasts, carried away by ships and by planes.

(otrā)

Sēžu, skatos, kā citi strādā, un klikšķinu matu sprādzi.
Ja nu tā būs mūžam, es nobīstos – aiz loga briest āboli, un nevis Jānītis dzer pienu [kā Ziedonim], bet domas šļakstās, nepamatoti izgaismojot zvaigžņu ceļus – brieduma nebūs? Neaizsniegšu? Pie vārtiem nepienāks? Klusēs un zvanīs
vien skatiens pār darba galdiem, pa vētras nostiepto stīgu, pa sniegputenī neapmaldīties ceļiem
atnāks, bet pa durvīm – neatnāks?

Ir nepareizi sēdēt tev blakus
klikšķināt to sprādzi, nezināt,
vai mēs vēl dzīvosim, vai šī jau ir otra puse,
ekrāna aizklātā nakts. Dienasgaismas spuldze padara ēnas plakanas.
Labvakar, Gogēna kungs. Jums pienācis pasts. Uz pastkartes lapu pavēnī kapara lapsa.

NEPAZĪSTAMĀ PARADĪZĒ

kā tevi meklēju nepazīstamā paradīzē
pat tur ir kā sapņos tu vienmēr sēdi ar muguru
katrreiz nevar pat atrast apavus
nevar sazīmēt kreklu lūdzu nevalkā neko rūtainu nekad nevelc svešas drēbes

tur rīgā es ar hemingveja lielo ķieģeli klēpī ilgi sēdēju rožu ielokā pie brīvības piemineklą
kāds zēns blakus dzēra sintētisku kakao kāda meitene steidzās acīmredzami apreibusi
kāds bundzinieks spēlējot ksilofonu miedza acis kā vērojot gaisa numurus cirkū

bet pa ieliektajām ietvēm pie brīvības pieminekļa
neviens pats negāja tavā gaitā
tad arī nobijos –
ja mēs dzīvotu pavisam citur
zem visiem tiem citrusiem mīdiju noklātiem galdiem jūras akmentiņiem un lidojošajām zivīm – matisa zili svelotajā debesī un akvareļu perioda jahtu dzeltenajās kajītēs

kā es tevi tur atrastu kā varētu zināt

vai tiešām mums tikai viens te parks viens piemineklis
brīvības
1 dzīve

(second)

Am sitting watching others work, clicking my hair clasp open and shut.
What if it's like this forever, the thought gives me a start – apples ripen outside, and it's not li'l Johnny drinking milk [as Ziedonis would have it], but thoughts splatter, lighting the pathways of stars –
no ripening for me? Will not get there? Will not knock on my door? Only some gaze will be silent or ring over the desks, will arrive across a rope strung by the storm, over roads not to get lost on in snowstorms but not through the door?

It is wrong to sit next to you,
clicking the hair clasp, not knowing,
if we have yet to begin living, or this is the other side,
night covered by screen. The strip light flattens the shadows.
Good evening, Mr. Gauguin. Here is your mail. A copper fox lurks on a postcard shielded by foliage.

AN UNKNOWN PARADISE

how i was searching for you in an unknown paradise
even there it's like in dreams you always have turned your back
even footwear can never be found
cannot spy where the shirt is please don't wear anything plaid never wear the clothing of others

back in riga i was sitting by the rose bushes near the freedom monument hemingway's huge volume in hand
next to me a boy was drinking synthetic cocoa a girl was in a hurry obviously lit up
a drummer was playing the xylophone squinting as if watching airborne circus acts

but on the curving pavements by the monument
no one was walking like you
that's when i got scared –
if we lived somewhere else
under all those citrus mussel covered tables sea pebbles and flying fish – in matisse's blue blazing sky and the yellow cabins of watercolour-period yachts
how would i find you there how would i possibly know

do we really have only one park here one monument
freedom
1 life

* * *

pamosties rudenī jūlijā pēdējā dienā
lietus notiesā vīrieša seju uz vēl vienu dienu

uz salas
nomirst Ingmars Bergmans
visas zemeņu lapas pulksteņi un nedrošie laivinieki aizver acis
līst tā it kā caurās plaukstas gribētu paņemt rokās to zemespleķi
bet ir tādi
kas skatās tieši pretī aukstajam karogam

melnbalti ilgi kadri

PĒC PLŪDIEM

pirmais tāds pavasaris pēc plūdiem –
nevienu reizi neredzu tevi piemiedzam acis.
sev apsolu aizbraukt uz jūru, bet pilnīgi gluds no manis pa gabalu atsakās
krasts.
tālākos laukos dīgst zāle kā puikām pirms brīvlaika apgriezti mati, tik stāva.
apslēpti kustīgs ir sīko kukaiņu skāviens tās ēnā.
nerādiet bērniem puķes, laistot dārzu, māca Žižeks, tās taču ir tik valšķīgas,
pieejamas.

plūdi nonesuši no flīzītēm visas dāmas. zirgi kā pieminekļi, balstā uz astes,
viena kāja uz svina lodes vai koka kastes – nav iespējams turēties kustībā,
tā jau kopš renesanses, nav iespējams turēt valdnieku bronzas mugurā
tikai uz divām.

koki iekrampējušies pilsētas muguras kaulā.
neredzu, kā pa to braukā caur stumbriem tavs gaismas sagrieztais augums.
strēles sāk pārdot uz stūriem papīros čaukstošos.
tu esi, tevis nav,
ar skrituļdēli kāds garām aizšauj, priecādamies par sauso zemi.

* * *

to wake up in autumn in july on the last day
the rain condemns a man's face to one more day

on an island
Ingmar Bergman has died
all strawberry leaves clocks and hesitant boatmen close their eyes
it is raining as if the torn hands wanted to pick up that piece of land
but there are those
who look straight at the cold flag

black-and-white slow frames

AFTER THE DELUGE

the first such spring after the deluge –
i do not see you squint once.
i promise myself to go to the sea, yet, perfectly smooth, the shore signals rejection.
in faraway fields grass sprouts like hair on boys cut before summer vacation, vertical. secretly lively is the embrace of small insects under its shadow.
do not show the kids flowers as you water the garden, says Žižek, they are so saucy, so easy.

the flood has carried all ladies off the tiles. horses like monuments, propped up on their tails
one hoof on a led cannonball or other detail – impossible to hold the movement, ever since renaissance, impossible to hold a king astride on bronze only on two legs.

trees digging their claws into the city's backbone.
i don't see through the trunks your body move turned by light.
streaks are being sold on street corners wrapped in rustling paper.
you are, you are not,
someone whizzes by on a skateboard, happy about the dry ground.

PĒDĒJĀS SARUNAS

1.

vēlreiz
par krunkām tavu
acu kaktiņos
kā izpletņa aukliņas
tās ceļ skatienu augšup
es ceļošu pa tevi
vēlreiz

2.

un šoreiz ar visu kā bija ar smaidu ar tulpēm pret gaismu
ar piedošanu vēlēšanos mūžīgi līgoties otra skatienā
kā vienīgajā šeit nokritušajā ezerā
nu labi vēlreiz
nesāksim visu no sākuma
esam pašā vidū
tikko izglābušies
atkal izrādījās
mūs kopj tie paši dārznieki
tās pašas vēsās lapas
nāc apaudz man apkārt
ietinamies
vēlreiz

3.

nav tas uzgleznojams
redzamais laiks ziedā kas noliek galvu uz tava galda
par šīm dienām
runājošām niknām ielām gar malām strauti pinas
sniega tērcēs dardedzes šķēpeles Alliksār
lūk viņa noliecas
gluda mīksta zaļām platām lapām
pret visu šo ledu
pret melnām malām
necaurredzamiem logiem
nav tas uzgleznojams
kā puķe nepanāk laiku bet laiks
puķi panāk

LAST CONVERSATIONS

1.

yet again
about the crow's feet in
the corners of your eyes
like parachute strings
they lift the gaze up
i will travel over you
yet again

2.

and this time with all the way it was with the smile with the tulips
toward the light
with forgiveness desire to always sway in the other's gaze
as the only lake around here
all right once again
let us not begin at the beginning
we are right in the middle
just barely escaped
and as it turned out
the same gardeners tend us
the same cool leaves
come grow around me
let us swaddle
once again

3.

it cannot be painted
the visible time in bloom resting its head on your table
over these days
over talking angry streets tangling streams
in the melting snows shards of rainbow showing Alliksaar
look she bends down
smooth soft with green broad leaves
against all this ice
against black edges
opaque windows
it cannot be painted
the flower failing to catch up with time but time
catching up with the flower

TAKSOMETRA RĀCIJA

par viņa asinsriti telpā liecina vien taksometra rācijā atskaņota mājas adrese. prom vai pie, atbrauc vai aizbrauc, nav zināms, tikai skaidrs, ka piestās pie vārtiem, tikai skaidrs, ka durvis aizvērsies, durvis aizvērsies un tas vienmēr kā uz atvadām sastingušais skatiens.
kā var cilvēks būt tik viens, viens tā kā telpa, par kuru jāmaksā vēl savus divdesmit piecus gadus.
nevar neko piebūvēt, nevar arī aizvērt un doties verandu Katmandu nomalē pirkt.
par viņa asinsriti telpā liecina adrese.
taksī varētu atstāt zīmīti:
„lai tev labi," jo simts punkti šis dzeltenais auto ir nākamais, kas tur brauks garām.
bet nav īstais gadsimts privātu labvēļu ziņām, un tīrā veidā ir divas iespējas kā to pateikt – pastiept pirkstus un piedot (un iemantot mirklīgu mieru) vai arī ar zobiem aiz cīpslu trosēm pievilkt cauri tumsai klāt gaišo miesu un plosīt, līdz rīts abus samaltos vieniniekus iekausē pavisam jaunā lietā, pasūta taksi uz staciju, pārdot kādam, kas nākamā mirklī šķērso nedrīkstot sliedes.

UZ LIDOSTU

tu it kā brauc uz lidostu man pakaļ
bet patiesībā sēdies taksī un brauc tikai atpakaļ
dūmi šoferim pīpējot sitas pret stiklu kā akvārijā
balss netrāpa telefonā trāpa tajā parkinga kartē
it kā uz lidostu
bet atpakaļ (amerika pārvēršas salā) savelkas dūrē
(gaisa atsvaidzinātājs cauri prērijai šūpojas fūrē)
pirksti ar ogli kāds zīmē to putnu no dzejoļa g. a. spirti nožūst
(arumi saritinās)
un izlīst tuša tev klēpī
neviens nekad nedzied par vīrieša klēpi
vēl vairāk bail vēl vairāk noslēpums
bet tādas domas var izdomāt gaisā

kilometri
vertikāli
starp mums

TAXI RADIO

the only evidence of his blood flow in space is the address pronounced on the radio. to or from, coming or going, no idea, can only be sure it will stop by the gate, can only be sure that the door will open and close and can only be sure of that gaze frozen as if always saying good-bye.
how can a person be so alone, alone as the space for which payments will have to be made for twenty-five years or so.
no additions to be built, no closing it and going to Katmandu to buy a veranda.
evidence of his blood flow in space is an address.
one could leave a note in the cab:
"take care," for a hundred percent this yellow car is the next one to pass by there.
but it is not the century for private well-wishers and there are only two ways to say it – stretch out your hand and forgive (earning instant peace) or to bite into the cables of veins to drag close the light flesh through the dark and tear at it until the morning blends the two ravaged loners into a completely new object and calls the taxi to the station to sell it to someone who at the very next instant crosses the tracks without being allowed.

TO THE AIRPORT

supposedly you're coming to the airport to get me
but in reality you get in a taxi and are going back
driver's cigarette smoke beats against the glass like in a fish tank
your voice does not hit the phone instead hits that parking slip
as if to the airport
but back (america becomes an island) making a fist
(truck's air freshener swings through the prairie mist)
coal smeared fingers someone drawing that bird from the g. a. alcools poem dry (fields rolling up)
and indian ink pours out all over your lap
no one ever sings about a man's lap
still more frightening still more secret
but such thoughts can be thought through in the air

kilometres
vertical
between us

* * *

man šķiet es iemīlēju sauju tavu sapņu
man šķiet tie sen sajaukušies ar maniem sapņiem
man šķiet mēs pašlaik riteņojam prom pa visiem ceļiem

guļam ar vēderiem smiltīs plūcam citronus taisām svilpītes
plēšam sandales kalnainu pilsētu akmens ejās

man šķiet mēs kaut kur aizbraukuši
atstājuši sev sīkas ogas
garajām vasaras brokastīm

noskūpsti mani tur tālumā
es saku no šejienes
nekustinādama lūpas

un tu noskūpsti mani
tur tālumā
nekustinādams lūpas

* * *

vai tiešām nepāries vai tiešām katru
pavasari lapās vīšos cauri parkam bērni pāri brauks
ar ratiņiem vai tiešām lielāks ir par mani vilnis
jā kara osta sagrauta cars bēdīgs noskatās

jā nepāries jo citādi es lēnām
pie krasta ledus plēksnēs pārvērstos
un bērnu pēdas skrienošās
man ausis izspertu
un klusums atnāktu un mēmums
(dzen betons saknes smiltīs
dzen ūdens delmus aizmirstos pret krastu)

bet augšpus nemitas dungāties ūdens būves dobuļos vecos
bet augšpus nemitas pienenes plaukt visos parkos
bet augšpus nemitas bērni atspoguļoties vīriešu vaigos
tie smejas par pirmo putnu gari pārstiepto dziesmu

* * *

I think I fell in love with a handful of your dreams
I think they've long since been mixed with mine
I think we're cycling off on every road

lying with our bellies in the sand plucking lemons making whistles
ruining our sandals on the stony passages of hilly towns

I think we have gone somewhere
having left just a handful of berries
for our long summer breakfasts

kiss me there far away
I say from here
without moving my lips

and you kiss me there
far away
without moving your lips

* * *

is it really not going to pass will I really
flutter through the park with leaves every spring and babies
will ride over me in strollers is the wave really bigger
yes the naval port's been destroyed the czar looks sadly on

no it will not pass otherwise I'd slowly
turn to sheets of ice by the shore
and the running feet of children
would kick out my ears
and silence would arrive and also muteness
(concrete drives roots in sand
water drives forgotten limbs to shore)

but above water keeps sloshing in old construction pits
but above dandelions keep opening in all parks
but above children keep mirroring themselves in cheeks of men
they laugh about the first bird-song stretched out way too long

ja es pārietu tās būtu beigas pēdējais bastions nobrukušas trepes
redzi es pati esmu
dunoņa betona saknēs klusēšana nemitīgajā jūrā
katru dienu sit rokas pret krastu
katru dienu betonā kliedziens
dzen zelta dzīslas

* * *

visās šīsdienas skicēs stūrī viens un tas pats nospiedums – uzdāvini mums žēlastību vēl mazliet maiguma nevar būt ka pavisam visi uz parīzi aizbraukuši nevar būt ka mūsu te nav atnācām taču un ēdienkartē pazuda izsalkušie skatieni
skaties tik sīka gaisma uz grīdas nokrīt krīts uz asfalta zīmē ielu neviens nezinātu kam piezvanīt piekļauties pierunāties klāt ja nebūtu sīko svītru prieks dusmas iekāre un smaidi gaismēnu sejās iešķībās

noliec atpakaļ mapi uz milimetru papīra sazīmēta iešana kam nav sava celiņa vienīgā skaņa klusums saliktajā pagātnē ko mēs varējām zināt es būšu bijis laimīgs tu teici šīsdienas debesīs ietriecoties pazaudējot jebkādas vadlīnijas kā dzīvot še tev topi pats sev par kladi uzdāvin-āšu tev zīmuli

* * *

Cik labi, ka tu esi mājās, es iedomājos. Man te ir klusums, un sajūta tāda, kā tad, kad ir tiešām septiņpadsmit gadu, un, skatoties draugu sejās, redzi šosejas aizšvīkstam acīs. Plūst ceļi, plūst baltās svītras un naktis, un rīti, kuru vēl nav, plūst runas, nekas netiek pateikts, brālis turpat. Mazais brālis, kurš dzird, kā tu smejies, pīpē, pumpurus gaidi un raudi. Kurš zina, ka maiznīcas smarža ap četriem no rīta ir tavas bantes, ko gludini, līdz iezogas gaisma. Tu vari visu dienu nēsāt tās līdzi.
Es nezinu, vai uz pleciem palika vieglā smarža. Zināšanas ir sīkas spuldzītes izmēģinājuma pultī fizikā. Uz sienas rakstīts: domā, bet viss ko tu proti – mīli. Vārds, ko slēpsi kā sataupītu visus nākamos gadus un tikai palaikam iekliegsies: arī mana „sirds ir smaga kā iespaidīgs Damaskas dāmas dibens”. Bet tobrīd tev tikai

if I passed that would be the end the last bastion decayed staircase
see I too am
booming in the roots of concrete silence in the relentless sea
every day hands beat against the shore
every day a scream drives
golden veins into the concrete

* * *

in all sketches of today there is one and the same imprint in the corner – give us some redemption a little more tenderness it cannot be that everyone has gone to paris it cannot be that we are not here we did come after all and our hungry glances were swallowed by the menu
look such faint light on the floor a piece of chalk falls on the pavement draw the street no one would know whom to call to snuggle to talk close if not for these tiny scratches joy anger desire and smiles in the crooked faces of chiaroscuro

put back the file on the millimetre paper walking drawn that does not have its own track the only sound silence in past perfect what could we have known I must have been happy you said crashing against today's sky losing any direction for living here be your own notebook I will give you a pencil

* * *

How nice that you are home, I suddenly thought. I have silence here and the kind of feeling that comes when you are really seventeen and, looking into the faces of friends, you see highways swish by in their eyes. Roads flow, the white lines and nights, and mornings yet to be flow, speech flows, nothing is said, brother's right there. Little brother who hears you laughing, smoking, waiting for bursting buds and crying. Who knows that the smell of the bakery around four in the morning is you ironing ribbons until light steals into the house. All day you can carry them along.
I don't know if the light smell remained on shoulders. Knowledge is tiny bulbs on an experiment board in physics. Writing on the wall: think; yet all that you know is – love. A word that you'll preserve like a treasure for all coming years just to yell out from time to time: "My heart meanwhile swells larger than the arse of a Damascan wife".

Nāzims Hikmets, putni un vieglas lūpas. Man patīk, kā tu smaržo
pēc vēja. Malku atnes. Atnes kokus, ar ko sasilt.
Noglāsti mani par visiem vakariem, rūgtām sliedēm un meža ceļiem.
Rokas ir putni, es esmu Nils Holgersons, mūžam es gribu tā ceļot.

IELA

pavasarī tas stūris izskatījās gaišāks
tu gāji tam garām redzams līdz pēdējam brīdim
ar jaunu seju ko nospriego pēkšņs maigums
tagad
iela uzgriezusi mums muguru
apsegusies ar cietām lapām

tu ieej pagriezienā
plāns kā akācijas svilpīte kas sāp pie lūpām
un pazūdi
jūlija tumsā kam pēkšņi ir novembra rokas

* * *

Es attapos guļam tāpat kā bērnībā
ar īkšķi piespiestu pie lūpām
– kā Žans Pols Belmondo –

aiz loga
it nekā
vairs nebija

migla bija iekrāvusi pilsētu čemodānā
visu pasauli čemodānā visus jrt godārus un hermaņus un
aiznesusi prom

tur kur no baltajām gubām barojas
daži reti koki kam plāns
uzziedēt atkal

But for the moment you have only Nazim Hikmet, birds and delicate lips. I like you smelling of wind. Bring in some firewood. Bring wood to get warm.
Caress me for the sake of all these nights, bitter rails and forest paths. Hands are birds, I am Nils Holgersson, I would like to travel like this forever.

STREET

in the spring that corner looked brighter
you passed it visible to the last moment
with a new face tense with a rush of tenderness
now
the street has turned its back
it has covered itself with sharp leaves

you make a turn
flat like an acacia pod whistle that hurts the mouth
and disappear
into the July darkness that suddenly has the arms of November

* * *

I found myself sleeping like a child
thumb pressed against my lips
– like Jean Paul Belmondo –

outside the window
there was
nothing at all

the fog had stuffed the city into a suitcase
the entire world into a suitcase including jrt[†] godard and hermanis[‡] and taken it away

to where you see feeding off the white drifts
a few sparse trees planning
to bloom once again

[†]*jrt*: Jaunais Rīgas teātris (New Riga Theatre) [‡]*Alvis Hermanis*: artistic director of JRT

bet es vairs nezināju
ne rītus vakarus nevienas pareizās taciņas
izeju uz āru bija nomainījušas tikai ieejas
durvju aplodas baltas kā sāpes

sapnī neatnāks neviens un pīpes dūmu arī
nepiedāvās
tev kļūs bail noticēt ka
– iespējams –

tik arī ir

tik āra
pasaules mala pie tava loga

tik klusuma
un ir jānoslāpst

tik miera
cik labprāt tu būtu dejojusi

tik vientulības
nekustīgas kā izplatījums

CITĀDI

mīlēt tas tomēr ir
kaut kā citādi.
ticēt pleciem un mugurai
tālumā ilgumā rāmumā.
visos gadalaikos
vērot to mierā un priekā
smaržot un pieskarties
tāpat kā ābelei aiz loga.
visos gadalaikos. sūrumā sāļumā
smaržā kas reizi vasarā atgriežas
apdāvināt mūs ar atmiņu.
dzidru. zaļajā zālē.

mīlēt citādi.
tas ir skatīties putekļos
gaidīt pārnākam mājās.

but I no longer knew
whether I was coming or going no true path
exits were all replaced by entrances
door jambs as blank as pain

no one will come in your dream nor will they offer
a smoke
you will fear the awareness that
  – possibly –

that is really it

that much of the outside
edge of the world by your window

that much silence
and you have to choke

that much peace
as you would have gladly danced

that much loneliness
motionless like the void

SOMETHING DIFFERENT

to love is
something different after all.
to believe in a pair of shoulders and a back
distance duration silence.
in all seasons
to observe it in peace and joy
to be fragrant and touch it
like the apple-tree outside the window.
in all seasons. in bitterness in saltiness
in fragrance that returns once every summer
to present us with memory.
lucid. in the green grass.

to love different.
that is looking through the dust
waiting for the homecoming.

rūgti raudāt kad aiziešana
ir vienīgais pareizais ceļš
bet uz zemes tā nav.

tikai grantēti ceļi kur bērns
skriedams apdauza kāju pirkstus
un ziedlapiņas līmē uz nagiem
tēlo princesi spēlē rūgtuma pilnu zvanu
kas attālinās.

citādi. atgriezties rītausmā mājās.
piespiesties siltam un miegainam plecam
jūtot ausīs šalkojam šosejas
un šķindam draugu balsis.

pamostoties
šķind vien monētiņas
par kurām viņš sestdienas pastaigā
nopirks ledenes –
krāsainos čemurus
ar kuriem var sagriezt mēli.

to cry bitterly when a departure
is the only appropriate way
but not on earth.

only gravel roads where a child
stubs its toes running
and sticks petals on fingernails
plays at princesses rings a bell of bitterness
receding.

different. to return home at dawn.
press against a warm and sleepy shoulder
feeling the swish of highways in ears
and the tinkle of friends' voices.

upon waking
just the tinkle of coins
on his Saturday walk he will use them
to purchase bonbons –
in colourful clumps
that can easily cut your tongue.

AGNESE KRIVADE

PHOTO: INGRĪDA PIČUKĀNE

AGNESE KRIVADE was born in 1981 in Riga. She has worked in public relations and advertising and was also a journalist. She is currently employed as a translator from English and German by the E.U. Committee of the Regions in Brussels. Krivade's reviews, essays and articles on cultural issues have appeared in a number of Latvian magazines and newspapers. Her first, visually highly inventive, collection of poetry, *Bērnība* (Childhood / Riga: Neputns), was published in 2007 and the majority of her poems in this selection have been chosen from that volume. Krivade has also published short stories.

COME, THEY TOLD ME

nāc tie man teica es nācu bet ceļā mani piekāva
cauri man tagad trauki ne nardu eļļas nav riekšavā
lienu pie Tevis uz priekškājām satriektiem lieliem asinīs plūzdams un
mušās zumēdams
nu ko varu dot? vien dārgāko to kas nav atņemts vienīgo pirkstu Tev
pierītē bakstīdams:
kāpēc jāmirst labāk paēd un paguli Bērniņ pa ra pa pa pam
nemīli mīlestību, neceri cerību, netici vispār vairs nekam
jo pirmkārt viss ir kā uz to skatās un otrkārt kā nu kuram cilvēkam

DIVI NAKTĪ

dāmas un kungi, jūs taču redziet, es esmu tik skaista un traģiska, ka nevar ne gulēt aiziet.

pasaki tik, ka tev nav gribējies mazo, ko likt uz vatītes čučēt ērkociņkastītē, kaltētu mušiņu pielikt blakus.

un teikt – nu čuči, duraciņ. redzi, kā kanālmalā cits citam uz pleca čuč balodis, pīle un mazā kaija. čuč uz palodzes kepons ar krūšturi aptinies. čuč tev podiņā kaka.

skaties, kā vasaras dzīvnieki, tumsu zīduši, silti un bēdīgi, nāk tev apkārt un glaužas, pūš savas zvēra elpas tev sejiņā, nāsītēs ložņā, sapnīšos iekšā ietiek.

arlabunakti, nu čučiet, dāmas un kungi, viens mazais man šonakt dzimis, par mazu, lai sauktu par bērniņu, bet man, teiksim, pietiek.

* * *

es varētu kaut ko nodziedāt
kādu komisku dziesmiņu
bet te vajag četrrocīgu pavadījumu uz klavierēm

COME, THEY TOLD ME

come they told me I came but was beat up along the way
my vessels are broken not even a drop of oil in my hand
I crawl to Thee on my forelegs my shins shattered covered in blood and buzzing with flies
what can I give? only what's most dear what hasn't already been taken the only finger tapping your forehead:
why die better eat and sleep Child pa rum pum pum pum don't love love, don't hope hope, believe in nothing at all
for first everything is as you look at it and second depends on who's talking

TWO A.M.

ladies and gentlemen, you see, don't you, I am so beautiful and so tragic, impossible to go to sleep.

sure, sure, you've never wanted a little one to put to sleep in a cotton-lined matchbox with a dried little fly beside.

and say – go to sleep, little munchkin, see how by the city canal, head on each other's shoulder, a pigeon, a duck, and the small sea-gull sleep, a cap enwrapped by a bra sleeps on the windowsill, your poo-poo sleeps in the potty.

how summer animals, suckled on darkness, sad and warm come around and press against you, blowing their beastly breaths in your face crawl through your pug nose, penetrate your dreams.

good night, please go to sleep, ladies and gentlemen, I have a little one born tonight, too tiny to call it a baby, but for me, it's enough, you know.

* * *

I could sing something
some funny song
but I'll need a four-handed piano

mans mīļākais gadalaiks, piemēram, ir ziema
tad var izlikties balts
un izlikties, ka ir biezas drēbes, lai gan patiesībā resns dibens

mans mīļākais gadalaiks pagājušajā gadā bija ziema
tad sēdēju pie tējas un turējos, lai nenokristu
nē, viss sajucis, vienkārši sildīju rokas

mans mīļākais un gadalaiks ir ziema
es nezinu, ko domāju, sakot, ka esmu pozitīvs
man, protams, ir smaidīga seja, bet ir arī dažādas infekcijas

gribētos, lai mīļākais gadalaiks ir ziema
tad varētu tēlot ka man ir tikai acis un mute
un nav dibena, deguna, Dieva un citu, kas salā piesarkst un nodod

tiešām, ziema kā gadalaiks ir diezgan mīļa
tiešām, tā es tagad gan dziedāšu
bet kāpēc jūs pie klavierēm sēžat ar līku muguru

* * *

grāmatu, kurā iekrist un pazust, kīnofilmu par lielām sāpēm
apmēram septiņas pēdējās dienas
piesnieg jūrmala, termoss ar karstvīnu, apelsīns kabatā
apmēram septiņas pēdējās dienas
labi, melnais balzams ar ledu, tievās cigaretes un vēl kaut kas normāls
vai tu saprati, kurā mirklī mēs pārtraucām runāt

vakar, nākot no darba, slīpi pārgāju visam pagalmam
drusku uzsnidzis, gaisma spīdēja mammītes logā
kāpēc tu guli zemē, pakrīti lūdzu uz manis, paglaudi mani, sniegs
šorīt tā kā saņēmos, tomēr pietika tikai pirmajai pusei
aizmigu, pamodos, aizmigu, redzēju vīru ar dažādām acīm
vienu šauru, bet otru – platu, kā izplēstu sejā ar spēku, redzēju
arī vienu ar tumšiem zobiem, salipinātiem biezām siekalām
tad vēl divus pēc urīna smirdošus maisiņos vācam vecrīgas sniegu,
    tad vēl citas nesmukas lietas

vai tevi netraucē tas, ka par tevi domāju
aizmirsu pieminēt tālu uguņu mirdzumu

my favourite season, for instance, is winter
for then one can pretend to be white
and pretend to have thick clothing even though it's just a fat ass

my favourite season last year was winter
I sat by my tea and tried to hold on not to fall
no, it's all mixed up, I just warmed my hands

my favourite and my season is winter
I don't know what I meant saying I was positive
I do have a smiling face but I also have a swarm of infections

I would like my favourite season to be winter
then I could pretend that I have only eyes and a mouth
and no ass, no nose, no God or others that flush in the cold and betray

winter as a season is really quite nice
now I really will sing
but why do you sit at the piano with your back so bent

* * *

a book in which to dive and get lost, a movie about some great pain
about the last seven days
seaside gets buried in snow, thermos with mulled wine, an orange in the pocket
about the last seven days
all right, black balsam with ice, thin cigarettes and some other normal thing
did you understand at what moment we ceased to converse

yesterday coming from work I crossed the yard on diagonal
a thin layer of snow, mummy's window was lit
why do you lie on the ground, fall a little on me, caress me a little, snow
this morning got sort of a grip on myself, yet there was enough only for
the first half
I fell asleep, awoke, fell asleep, awoke, saw a man with different eyes
one was narrow the other wide as if forced open in his face, I saw
also one with dark teeth covered with thick saliva
and another two reeking of urine collecting the old town snow in bags,
then some other ugly things

are you not bothered by the fact that I am thinking of you
I forgot to mention the distant glow of lights

varbūt pāriet šaurākās vietās, varbūt no tevis uz tēju ar citronu
vai tu saprati, kurā mirklī mēs pārtraucām runāt
varbūt atsākt klausīties pleijeri, varbūt kaut kādu kīnofilmu par sāpēm
vēlreiz izgudrot visas šīs pilsētas vietas
pilsēta – silta kakao lāse, lejup no sestā stāva
no kakla pār visu muguru
apmēram septiņas pēdējās dienas

* * *

kāpēc neviens mani neņem vētrā
smaržoju benzīna nogulsnēs līzdama

atkal pie precīzām formām un taisnām līnijām bučoties
nē, es šitā vairs nevaru

ķirmji un mati nāk ārā, bet paliek virsū un nenorit
sīkas bēdiņas izpil no pārgrieztas rokas

sīkās bēdiņās saslapis zīmējas rīts
celies

manā vietā uz tava pakauša tumsa

indes pīrādziņš
eņģeļu kaulu miltos
apvārtīts

* * *

kliedziens
autogrāfs
kliedziens
autogrāfs

kurā vietā
tu strādā par sūdu

perhaps I should move to narrower spaces, perhaps from you to tea with lemon
did you understand at what moment we ceased to converse
perhaps I should resume listening to the player, perhaps some movie on pain
again invent all the places in this city
the city – a warm drop of cocoa, down from the sixth floor
from the neck over the entire back
about the last seven days

* * *

why does nobody take a dance with me
I am fragrant crawling into the gasoline sediment

to kiss again by precise forms and straight lines
no I can't do it like this

wood-borers and hair come out but stay on and do not fall
little sorrows drop out of a cut hand

soaked in little sorrows the morning draws out
get up

in my place there is darkness at your nape

a poisoned pie
dredged in angel
bone dust

* * *

a scream
an autograph
a scream
an autograph

where is it that
you work as a shit

kur tu laipni
luncini ārprātu

kam tu šobrīd
sagrauzdē plecu

cik jāsamaksā
par pelnu delnā

cik maksā izdzēst autogrāfu no visu pusložu virsmām, cik maksā nenovītušas ausis, cik maksā mēle roku dzelžos, cik saplēstais audums uz pirkstu galiem
cik fucking pienākošs pavasaris, cik neķītri plaukuši bērzu zari, cik maksā pirksts uz durvju zvana, cik pilnīgi tava man pazušana

* * *

ko darīt cilvēkam Rīgā
agri no rīta
staidzinot cauri bulvāriem pūdeli,
vai arī tas ir kaķēns, vai arī neveiksmīgs pasākums
atbildi, nakts

sabirzt papusei pulverī pūdelis
rīta migla kā pelējums pazodē
pasaki, pilsēta, kā ir jālieto bulvāris
kur te ir atļauts
apstāties, apdzīt, rakt

es un pulverī sabirzis pūdelis
bulvārus pazīž no mazās pudeles
paplosa pasaules vaļējos kanālos
vai šeit jebkad maz
ir bijis tik agrs

sen jau mēs besījam ārā šo bulvāri
iekaisīt pūdeli pilsētai acīs,
iekaist no pastaigas pilsētai bulvāris
klusē pulveris runā Rīga
un runā nakts

where you kindly
wag your lunacy

you presently toast
whose shoulders

how much is
an ash in a dash

how much does it cost to erase an autograph from all surfaces, how much do unhurt ears cost, how much a tongue in handcuffs, how much the torn fabric on fingertips
how fucking arriving the spring, how lewd the birch branches have burst in leaf, how much does a finger on the doorbell cost, how totally your disappearing to me

* * *

what can a person do in Riga early in the morning
walking a poodle down the boulevards,
or perhaps it's a kitten or a failed event
answer me, night

the poodle half crumbles to dust
morning fog like a mouldy chin
tell me, city, how does one use a boulevard
where one is allowed
to stop, overtake, dig

me and a poodle crumbled to dust
suck the boulevards from the small bottle
tear at world's open canals
has it even been here
so early ever

we've been vexing this boulevard long
to pour poodle in city's eyes
from the walk boulevard gets inflamed
powder keeps quiet, Riga speaking
and the night also speaking

LEDUSSKAPĪ

paņem vienu vārītu olu, mazais.
tā visilgāk no visa tur ļaunu prātu, gan siltu, gan aukstu.
paskaties spogulī, atzīsties: diemžēl palīdzēt nevaru.

paņem arbūza pusi un saplosi.
izruikā, asinīm noplūzdams, izplēs kā vilciņš stirniņai sānu.
tā, lūk, atriebies mammai un tētim par bērnības traumām, vēlāk pasaki "joks".

paņem un sāc kaut kā dzīvot, mazais. balsties uz patiesiem notikumiem.
izņirdz visu ar to, ka eksistē, vai pat ar muti.
kad pamosties, neraudi, vārītas oliņas nebūs vairs blakus.
kad pamosties, neraudi, ledusskapī tik es. viena pati.

* * *

ļoti jūtu
manī notiek
ierēdņi un pārpratumi

pilsētas
uz kurām raugos
pārvēršas par polārlapsām

radio saka
tagad visur
ejot sudrabainas līnijas

nu tad lūk
viena tieši
tagad iet
man caur roku

MĀJAS

*

ar laimi šais mājās vairāk vai mazāk kārtībā
pieceļas katrs otrais, kam šādi paliku parādā

LIVING IN THE FRIDGE

take one boiled egg, little one,
that keeps anger longer than anything, warm or cold,
look in the mirror, confess: unfortunately it cannot be helped

take a watermelon half and tear it up
ravage it, getting covered with blood, tear out like a wolf the side of a deer
take this revenge on mummy and daddy for your childhood trauma, then say
it's a joke

take it and get some kind of life, buddy, base it on real events
ridicule it all with your very existence or even with your mouth
when you wake up, don't cry, there won't be any boiled egg
when you wake up, don't cry, in the fridge there's just me. all alone.

* * *

I feel it strongly
it's happening
bureaucrats and misunderstandings

cities
that I look at
turn into polar foxes

radio says
now everywhere
silvery lines are stretching

so look
one just
now is passing
through my hand

HOME

*

in terms of happiness it's more or less ok at this house
every other one to whom I owe this is raising their hand

es tomēr varētu ieslēgt radio, uzvilkt halātu, iekosties ābolā
varētu celties, ja atnāktu kāds, kas no palaga atpogā
piemēram katrs otrais, kam šādi paliku parādā

*

sēžot uz cilvēka stumbra šaipusē atnāca vaļā acis
pietrūkst politiskas gribas
pavērt mēteli, gavilēt vai arī vēl ko te sacīt
tikai līdz pusei apzinos personisko traģēdiju un arī to tik līdz pusei
gribētos citreiz teikt: kur viņa ir, vai kāds viņu jūt
es jūtu tikai, ka tūlīt būs sūdi
ir pagalmos jāiet bet piepogāts palagam nevaru pat ne pusi
the page can not be displayed
viņš nevar atvērt to lappusi
nedz arī klusēt

* * *

meklē vieglumu, mīļais? nemeklē mani
meklē bālganus zirneklīšus
putekšņus bitīšu saņurcītus

iestāsti sev kādu ziedošu mauriņu
padzer no vārnas, no skudras vai cita, kas visu var
aizstaigā debešos, savērpies viesulī, redzi, kā lieli

skaistums un žēlums visu pasauli ar

RUDENS

iesaku atteikties no draugiem
kad viņi sāk smaržot pēc trūdošām lapām
vai arī visam būs vilkties vēl vienas cigaretes garumā
lietus, kas satriec lielus, sašķaida potītes, saēd lūpas
nogāž gar zemi, izlauž lāpstiņas, izvārta dubļainos arumos

laime, kas ceļas virs meža, kamēr tu nirsti ezerā
blakus peld čūska un viņai ir zvīņu ēde visā garumā
kaija, kas aizskrien mums pāri ar ķieģeli knābī
lūdzu pasaki viņiem, lai ņem mani labāk par pavasari

I could turn on the radio put on a bathrobe bite into an apple
could get up if anyone who could unbutton the sheet came over
for instance every other one to whom I owe this

*

sitting on a man's trunk on this side eyes came open
political will is lacking
to open the coat cheer or say something more
I'm half aware of my personal tragedy but only half
sometimes would like to say where is it does anyone feel it
I only feel that I'm about to be up shit creek
I have to go out but buttoned to a sheet I can't even halfway
the page cannot be displayed
he cannot open that page
nor can he keep quiet

* * *

looking for easy, my love? don't look for me
look for pale little spiders
pollen dust worked over by bees

tell yourself a blossoming lawn
drink from a crow, from an ant or from anyone who can it all
go to the skies, twist in a storm, see how the big ones

beauty and grace plough over the globe

AUTUMN

my advice is to get rid of friends
when they begin to smell of rotting leaves
or it will all have to drag on the length of another cigarette
rain that shatters shins, smashes ankles, corrodes lips
throws to the ground, breaks shoulder blades, rolls in the muddy field

happiness that rises above the forest while you dive in the lake
a snake swims beside you and it has psoriasis the length of it
sea-gull, you that fly over us brick in beak,
please tell them I'd rather they took me for spring

VASARA

neteiksim, protams, ka man būtu bail no lapsenes
tomēr šoruden atkal jūtos tik sīka
pilsēta agri man pagrieza asu pakausi
izlauza rokas un atņēma darbarīkus

veca šovakar, pilsēta, tava vasara
pasaki viņām, pilsēta, arī par mani
izdzeriet taču kokteiļus savus meitenes
pirms tos izlaiza gurdās vasaras lapsenes

bet viņas sēž; kā mīkstās mantiņas; lielām, tramīgām acīm; sejām dzeltenā smiņķī; kā pura velli; un skatās; sienās, gleznās, skatās tavās rokās; rauc pieri, spoguļojas šķiltavās; tai brīdī kamera pievelk tuvāk tavu seju; tu esi cits; tu, iespējams, raudi; nu protams, tāda milzu mīlīga meiteņu varza, kaut kāds ārprāts; laikam būtu jāceļas un jāiet; bet lapsenes, bet tās lapsenes, lapsenes, baby; visas pudeļu maliņas apskretušas; visas glāzītes pilnas piekritušas; mojito, sex on the beach, daiquiri, strawberry margarita, white russian; mērcē; deguntiņus, dibentiņus mērcē, kamēr iekritušas; kamēr visu izdzērušas; uz tava rēķina, vienmēr tava; un ja tev liksies, ka man vienkārši skauž; jā; mierīgi, ir okei, bet rītrītā modīsies trīcošs un agresīvs
mīkstu, salduma savilgušu
pēdējo vasaras lapseni mutē

* * *

viņa ir melnā mežģīņu krūšturī ķerdama krītošas spalvas
viņa ir skaista

tu sēdi sniega cietoksnī pīpē un smaidi
vakars iespiests starp kalsnām un tumšām ciskām
vakars sabriedis divreiz lielāks kā galva

sēžam siltā kakao līdz potītēm, brīdī
kad iedegas gaisma, tu vērsies pie manis un saki
tu pat nesmaidi, baby

SUMMER

it's not exactly that I am afraid of the wasp
yet this autumn I feel little again
the city turned a sharp back to me early
dislocated my arms and took away tools

it is old this evening, city, your summer
tell them, city, also for me
drink up your cocktails, girls
before they're licked up by lazy summer wasps

but they sit there; like soft toys; with big, skittish eyes; with faces in yellow make-up; like banshees; and stare; at walls, pictures, stare at your hands; frown; examine their reflection in the lighter; at that moment the camera draws near to your face; you are some one else; you quite possibly are crying; well, naturally, such a string of cute girls, what horror; probably should get up and go; but for these wasps, baby, these wasps, these wasps; all bottle necks grimy; all glasses full of the fallen; mojito, sex on the beach, daiquiri, strawberry margarita, white russian; they dip; they dip their noses, dip their butts until they fall in; until they've drunk it all; on your penny, always yours; and if it seems to you that I am simply envious, yeah; sure thing, it's okay, but next morning you'll wake trembling and aggressive with a soft, sweetness filled
wasp
summer's last wasp in your mouth

* * *

she is in a black lacy bra catching falling feathers
she is beautiful

you sit in a snow fortress smoking and smiling
the evening pressed between dark skinny thighs
the evening ripened twice as big as the head

we are sitting in hot cocoa up to our ankles, at the moment
when it lights up, you turn to me and say
you're not even smiling, baby

MARTS PUJĀTS

PHOTO: AUTHOR'S ARCHIVE

MARTS PUJĀTS was born in 1982 in Ikšķile. Having received a rigorous musical training at Riga's famous Dom Choir School where he was considered to be an exceptionally talented musician, he has been earning his living in advertising and working on his poetry. Pujāts made his debut as a poet in 1988 and has since published two books of poetry *Tuk tuk par sevi* (Knock Knock for Myself / Riga: Pētergailis, 2000) and *Mūsu dziesma* (Our Song / Riga: p-art, 2006). His poetry has also been translated into several languages, including a book *Two-Star Churches* published in Russian in 2005.

1.

es atgriežos istabā ar pīķa caurdurto sirdi
es atgriežos istabā ar tiesneša ķēdi
ar tālskati vecu
ar pīpi un pīpes rīkiem
tālāk jūtu plikas vecenes klātbutni
kaut kur aiz grāmatu plauktiem
plikas vecenes klātbūtni kaut kur erotiskajās kārtīs un mīkstos vākos
ar pīķa caurdurtu sirdi
ar tiesneša ķēdi
ar tālskati vecu
ar pīpi un pīpes rīkiem
kaut kur aiz plauktiem kārtīs un vākos

2.

es atgriežos istabā ar maizes kasti
es atgriežos istabā ar auksto skapi
ar vaskadrānu vecu
ar nazi un trinamiem rīkiem
tālāk jūtu plikas vecenes klātbūtni
kaut kur aiz kastroļiem
plikas vecenes klātbūtni kaut kur galda piederumos un dzeltenā mikserī
ar maizes kasti
ar auksto skapi
ar vaskadrānu vecu
ar nazi un trinamiem rīkiem
kaut kur aiz kastroļiem piederumos un mikserī

3.

es atgriežos istabā ar rūtainu segu
es atgriežos istabā ar žuburu lustru
ar lūpeni vecu
ar šķērītēm un līdzīgiem rīkiem
tālāk jūtu plikas vecenes klātbūtni
kaut kur aiz stūra dīvāna
plikas vecenes klātbūtni kaut kur putekļu mēteļos un izbāztā putnā
ar rūtainu segu
ar žuburu lustru

1.

I return to the room with a skewered heart
I return to the room with a judge's chain
with old binoculars
with a pipe and pipe fixtures
and then I feel the presence of a naked broad
somewhere behind the bookshelves
the presence of a naked broad somewhere among the erotic cards and
  between soft covers
with a skewered heart
a judge's chain
old binoculars
with a pipe and pipe fixtures
somewhere behind the bookshelves among cards between covers

2.

I return to the room with a bread box
I return to the room with a cold closet
with and old oilcloth
with a knife and sharpening tools
and then I feel the presence of a naked broad
somewhere behind pots and pans
the presence of a naked broad somewhere among kitchen utensils and
  a little yellow mixer
with a bread box
with the cold closet
with an old oilcloth
with a knife and sharpening tools
somewhere behind pots and pans among utensils and in mixer

3.

I return to the room with a checkered blanket
I return to the room with a branched chandelier
with an old lipstick
with nail scissors and similar instruments
and then I feel the presence of a naked broad
somewhere behind the corner sofa
the presence of a naked broad somewhere among the dust jackets and
  a stuffed bird
with a checkered blanket
with a branched chandelier

ar lūpeni vecu
ar šķērītēm un līdzīgiem rīkiem
kaut kur aiz stura putekļos un putna

* * *

baznīcām torņu vietā bija akas kurās es spaiņos laidu lejā tūristus
uz leju tie gāja smagi uz augšu viegli
uz augšu tie nāca viegli un tukši
tukšajos kāpa iekšā tūristi
uz leju tie gāja smagi uz augšu tukši
un tad reiz uznāca augšā spainis kas nebija gluži tukšs –
spaiņa dibenā pie auklām kāds bija aizmirsis kapeiku turētāju

* * *

būdams pēdējā maizē iegriezos no skata necilā vulkāniskas
    izcelsmes būdā
tur mani laipni sagaidīja melnais dūmotājs
un lika mani uz marmora lāvas
apgājās kā ar maizi
viņš lauza mani publiskajā turku pirtī
mirkli aiz Bēringa šauruma
un nerunāja kā nerunā kad paliek viens
un beigās ar mani kā ar maizi fotografējās
it kā es būtu gatavs nevis relaksējies un tīrs
it kā es būtu liekams galdā nevis aicināms pie tā

with an old lipstick
with nail scissors and similar instruments
somewhere around the corner in the dust and in bird

* * *

the churches had wells instead of spires and I let tourists down in buckets
they were heavy going down light coming up
up they came empty and weightless
the tourists climbed into the empty ones
they were heavy going down empty coming up
and then one time a bucket came up that was not completely empty –
in the bottom by the ropes someone had forgotten the penny counter

* * *

down to my last crumb of bread I stopped by a seemingly ordinary shack
of volcanic origin
where I was greeted kindly by the black smoker
who put me on a marble shelf
treated me like bread
he broke me in the public Turkish baths
a moment past the Bering Straits
and did not speak as one does not when one is alone
and finally he took pictures with me loaf-of-bread-like
as if I was ready instead of well-rested and clean
as if I was about to be put on the table instead invited to it

* * *

Caur Sapņojumu[1]
Caur Dusmām kuras neesot[2]
Caur Sapni kurā asras līstot[3]
    kur pirmo reizi klusēšana[4] atzīta par zeltu
Caur Pastaigu[5]
un Kiarīnas[6] ritmizētiem[7] glāstiem
nāk meistars Raro[8]
kritiķis[9] un ne tas gaisīgākais

Tad lūk šim kungam kurš visu mūžu dzīvoja ap pašizdomāto doktoru Raro
pašizdomāto Pastaigu
un vēl pāris citiem sevis variantiem
bij sieva ar gaišiem matiem[10]

Un šī sieva bij draudzene kādam citam kungam[11]
    kam pašizdomātais ceciliānisms[12] bij pieņemamākais no visiem
        sevis variantiem

Tad lūk šo sievieti ar gaišiem matiem
es gribu sev

[1] 'Sapņojums': vācu komponista Roberta Šūmaņa (*Schumann,* 1810-1856) klavieru skaņdarbs no cikla *Albuma lapas* (1840).
[2] 'Man dusmu nav': R. Šūmaņa dziesma no vokālā cikla *Dzejnieka mīla* (1840).
[3] 'Man sapnī asras lija': dziesma no tā paša cikla.
[4] Dziesmā 'Man sapnī asras lija' pirmoreiz mūzikas vēsturē pauze tiek lietota kulminācijas sasniegšanai.
[5] 'Pastaiga': R. Šūmaņa skaņdarbs klavierēm no cikla *Karnevāls* (1835).
[6] 'Kiarīna': skaņdarbs no tā paša cikla.
[7] Skaņdarbs ir pietiekami ritmizēts.
[8] 'Meistars Raro': skaņdarbs no cikla *Karnevāls.*
[9] Ar pseidonīmu Meistars Raro R. Šūmanis parakstīja savas filozofiski ievirzītās recenzijas (romantiski apcerīgās recenzijas viņš parakstīja ar pseidonīmu Eizēbijs, negatīvās – ar pseidonīmu Florestāns).
[10] Klāra Šūmane-Vīka (Schumann Wieck, 1819-1896): vācu komponiste un pianiste.
[11] Johaness Brāmss (Brahms, 1833-897), vācu komponists.
[12] Atgriešanās pie Romas polifonās mūzikas ievērojamākā pārstāvja Palestrīnas mūzikas tradīcijām.

* * *

Through Träumerei [1]
Through the Anger that there is none of [2]
Through the Dream in which tears flow [3]
        Where for the first time silence is the weight of gold [4]
Through the Stroll [5]
and rhythmical [6] caresses of Chiarina [7]
comes Master Raro [8]
critic [9] not the ephemeral kind

So this gentleman who lived all his life around the self-styled Dr. Raro
the self-invented Stroll
and a couple of other variations of self
had a wife with light hair [10]

And this wife was the girlfriend of another gentleman [11]
to whom his self-invented Cecilianism [12] was the most acceptable
        of his variations of self

Well, this very woman with light hair
I would like to have.

[1] 'Träumerei': a piano composition by German composer Robert Schumann (1810-1856) from *Albumblätter* (1840).
[2] 'I Have No Anger': Schumann's song from the *Dichterliebe* cycle (1840).
[3] 'Tears Were Flowing in My Dream': a song from the above cycle.
[4] In the song 'Tears Were Flowing in My Dream', for the first time in the history of music a pause is used to reach a culmination.
[5] 'Stroll': Schumann's composition for the piano from the cycle *Carnaval* (1835)
[6] The composition is quite rhythmical.
[7] 'Chiarina': a composition from the above cycle.
[8] 'Master Raro': a composition from the above cycle.
[9] Schumann used the pseudonym Master Raro to sign his philosophical reviews (the romantically brooding reviews he signed with the pseudonym Eusebius and the negative ones with the pseudonym Florestan).
[10] Clara Schumann Wieck (1819-1896): German composer and pianist.
[11] Johannes Brahms (1833-1897): German composer.
[12] Return to the musical tradition of the most outstanding representative of Roman polyphonic music, Palestrina.

* * *

ieiet tevī no sētas puses
kur atsliets vecais velosipēds, spainis ar lietus ūdeni
iebuktēts auto
suns mežonīgi rej
stāvi klusu
plūmes lēnām bojājas nepļautajā pagalma zālē
kur suns mežonīgi rej un tramīgs
it kā paredzētu zemestrīci
kur atsliets vecais velosipēds, spainis ar lietus ūdeni
žūst veļa, mitrs betons, gumijas āmurs tapām
suns mežonīgi rej
teicu mierā
kur atsliets vecais velosipēds, spainis ar lietus ūdeni
plūmes lēnām bojājas nepļautajā pagalma zālē
suns mežonīgi gaudo
it kā paredzētu saimnieka nāvi
kur žūst veļa, mitrs betons, gumijas āmurs tapām
auklā karājas lapseņu slazds

* * *

Ienākusi savā dzīvoklī, Kristele nez kāpēc uz plauktiņa ieraudzīja zilonilejkannu. Nē, to, ka ir tāds zilonis, viņa zināja, bet to, ka viņam ir acs, to Kristele nebija piefiksējusi.

Viņa ielūkojās lejkannas acī, nu, nekā tur nav – nedzīva acs, acs, kas ir vaļā, bet neskatās.

Nu, bet nekas, man tik un tā šī acs patīk. Viņai ir sava izteiksme. Tā nav suņa paklausīgā acs un nav kaķa nepaklausīgā acs. Tā ir ziloņa acs, ziloņa, kas pazīst un maigi ar snuķi aptausta savu mirušo senču kaulus.

* * *

jebkurš klusums ir kā naktī robežpunktā apstājies autobuss
jebkurā kusuma brīdī kāpj iekšā robežsargi ar savām dīvainajām micēm
klusuma ir kā naktī pļavā avarējusi vieglā automašīna
kuras augšupvērstie riteņi pamazām pārstāj griezties

* * *

to enter you through the back door
where the old bicycle is propped up, where there is a bucket with rain water
a banged up car
a dog barking wildly
would you shut up
plums slowly rotting in the unmown grass
where a dog barks wild and skittish
as if predicting an earthquake
the old bicycle is propped up, a bucket with rain water
laundry drying, damp concrete, a rubber hammer for pegs
dog barking wildly
I said shush
where the old bicycle is propped up, a bucket with rain water
plums slowly rotting in the unmown grass
dog howling wildly
as if predicting his human's death
where laundry is drying, damp concrete, a rubber hammer for pegs
a wasp trap dangling on string

* * *

Entering her apartment, Christelle for some reason noticed an elephant watering can. Yes, she did know there was such an elephant, it just hadn't registered that he had an eye.
She looked into the eye of the watering can – well, nothing really: a dead eye, an eye that is open but does not look.
But that's okay, I still like this eye. It has its own expression. It is not the obedient eye of a dog and it is not the disobedient eye of a cat.
It is the eye of an elephant: an elephant that knows and, with his trunk, touches gently the bones of his dead ancestors.

* * *

any silence is like a bus stopped in the middle of the night at a border post
in any silence border guards climb in with their strange hats
silence is like a car at night in a field after an accident
its upside down wheels gradually ceasing to turn

cilvēki ar kabatas baterijām nāk noskaidrot vai kāds nav cietis
un tad izsauc attiecīgos dienestus

kad mājīgs milzīgs autobuss naktī apstājas pie pēdējā luksofora
kas savieno pilsētu ar neitrālo zonu
iestājas viegli personificējams klusums
tāds kurš klātesošs dzīvās un jautrās vakara sarunās
tāds kurš liek sapnī skriet uz vietas
viņš jums skaidri pateiks kas šodien par prelūdiju un fūgu
kur šobrīd pastaigājas misters bīns
kā jau jebkurš klusums

tas paliek krustojumā un izaug par dzīvu un jautru pilsētu
kad mājīgais milzīgais autobuss uzsāk savu gaitu pie zaļās gaismas
un meitenes skatoties pa aizmugures logu pie sevis sauc
ardievu minka

* * *

Kristele un Ežēns staigāja pa mazu kūdras racēju pilsētiņu ar nevajadzīgi platām ielām skaidrā ziemas rītā.
Priekšā daudz sliežu, uz tām vagoni ar rupjā maluma kūdru.
Bija jālien un bija jāparādās zemessargam lauka formā.
Stāt – uzkliedza divu bērnu tēvs – (dēls Haralds iet tēva pēdās – māk salikt Makarova tipa pistoli, meita Jana baro jūrascūciņu Hruščovu) – kur lienat?
Abi pagriezās un neizpratnē apskatīja prātā vājo.
Pieliekusies Kristele jautāja Ežēnam ausī – kāpēc tas tērētais pimpis tēmē uz mani ar piku?

* * *

Kristele un Ežēns bija atlaidušies viņnedēļ pļautā zālienā uz dvieļa.
Vai tu zini – Kristele ievaicājās, grozīdama rokās petangas lodi – kāpēc puiku balsis sauc par eņģeļu balsīm?
Nu, laikam… – Ežēns pieslējās pussēdus, lai mēģinātu atbildēt, bet Kristele turpināja:
Tā taču viņas sauc, vai ne? Bet tas taču sanāk ar kājām gaisā. Kāds

people with flashlights come to see if anyone's hurt
and then call the authorities

when a huge cosy bus stops at night by the last traffic light
that connects the city to no-man's land
an easily personified silence sets in
silence that is present at lively and gay evening talk
silence that makes one run in place in a dream
it will tell you exactly what there is for a prelude and fugue today
where exactly strolls mister bean
as any silence would

it remains at the intersection and grows into a lively and gay city
when the huge cosy bus starts up at the green light
and girls looking through the back window call out to themselves
farewell kitty-cat

* * *

Cristelle and Eugene walked through a small peat-mining town with unnecessarily wide streets on a clear winter morning.
Many rails ahead, railway cars on the rails with coarse-ground peat.
They had to crawl under and a home guard in field uniform had to appear.
Stop – shouted the father of two – (the son, Haralds, takes after his father – knows how to put together a Makarov-type gun; the daughter, Jana, tends a guinea pig by the name of Khrushchev) – where are you going?
The two turned around and puzzled looked at the dimwit.
Leaning forward, Cristelle whispered into Eugene's ear: – why is that nutty asshole aiming a snowball at me?

* * *

Cristelle and Eugene were lying down on a towel spread on a lawn mown a week ago.
"Do you know", Cristelle asked, playing with a petanque ball, "why boys' voices are called the voices of angels?"
"Well, probably..." Eugene rose to a half-sitting position to attempt an answer, but Cristelle continued:
"That's what they are called, aren't they? Whereas it's the other way

ietekmīgs kungs izdzirdēja puiku dziedāšanu un iedomājās, ka tā varētu dziedāt eņģeļi, bet pēc tam tiek pieņemts, ka eņģeļi JAU tā dzied, un puikas dzied kā eņģeļi, bet patiesībā eņģeļi ir tie, kas, ja tādi vispār ir un ja dzied, tad dzied kā puikas, nevis otrādi.
Nu, tu jau pati esi tagad atbildējusi uz savu jautajumu.
Bet tu man pasaki, kas tajās puiku balsīs ir tāds?
Tur ir...
Bet Kristele pārtrauca:
Puiku balsis ir taisnas. Lūk, tur meklējams to pievilcīgums. Tās nav kā operdziedātājām – AaAaAaA – viņa atdarināja operdziedātāju vibrato – puikām nekā tāda nav. Puiku taisnās balsis – lūk, dabā nekur nesastopamā tikai abstrakti iedomājamā taisnā līnija, lūk, absolūti melns objekts – un Kristele paripināja Ežēnam petangas lodi.

* * *

Man zvanīja režisors,
Kurš vēloties parādīt saviem studentiem dzīvu dzejnieku mācību nolūkos.

Jau reiz tiku rādīts studentiem,
Kad mani kā divus mēnešus vecu, zilu zīdaini operēja.

Tagad pasakiet, vai šeit ir velkamas kādas paralēles,
Vai, vēl ļaunāk, koncentriski apļi.

* * *

Mēs bijām atlaidušies pie baznīcas zemā mūrīša un tērzējām par senām valodām un senām rakstībām.
Tikko bija uzsnidzis daudz un slapjš.
Gar baznīcas malu uz mūsu pusi uz šaurām un garām, un sarkanām slēpēm tuvojās divi aizkaros tērpti ērmi no Turīnas ziemas spēlēm.
Tie piesēž uz mūrīša, galvas kā lustras.
Mans biedrs tiem prasa: Iedo padzerties.
Viens ērms atbild: a par ko jūs tur runājat un kas jums tur slapjajā sniegā stāv rakstīts.
Mēs runājam – saku – par senajām mēlēm, un tur tajā sniegā mans biedrs ar nūju ir rakstījis vārdu sendienu fontā.

round. Some influential gentleman heard the boys singing and thought that that's how angels would sing, and after that it's assumed that angels DO sing like that and boys sing like angels, whereas in fact angels – if there are any and if they sing – sing like boys, not the other way round.
Well, now you have answered your own question.
But tell me what is it in these voices?
There is…
Yet Cristelle interrupted:
"Boys' voices are straight. That's their attraction. They are not like opera divas': AaAaAaA," and she imitated an opera singer's vibrato, "the boys have nothing of the kind. The straight voices of boys – here is your straight line that you can never encounter in nature but only think of abstractly, here is your absolutely black object," and Cristelle rolled the petanque ball over to where Eugene sat.

* * *

A theatre director called me up
He wanted to show his students a living poet for education purposes.

Once I've already been shown to students
When I was operated on as a blue two-month-old.

So tell me, should any parallels be drawn here
Or, even worse, concentric circles.

* * *

We were resting by the low wall of a churchyard conversing about ancient languages and ancient writing.
It had just snowed a lot, and wet.
By the side of the church, on long, skinny, red skis, two curtain-wrapped freaks from the Turin winter games were approaching.
They sat down on the wall, heads like chandeliers.
My buddy says: gimme a drink.
One of the freaks says: but what were you talking about and what is that writing in the wet snow.
We were talking, says I, about the old tongues and there in the snow my buddy has written a word in an ancient script with a stick.

Otrs ērms vaicā: a ko tas senais vārds nozīmē.
Tam nozīmju – saku – vairāk kā vajag, tas izslēdz laiku un stīgā savērpj ikdienas dzīvi, bet pa lielam tas nozīmē *tagad.*
Un vēlreiz ērms tincina: a darbā jums nav jābūt?
Mēs abi kopā: nē.
To dzirdot ērms pasniedz man pudeli. Tur iekšā ne vairāk par vienu piekto. Es rāvienā tukšoju izpūsto stiklu un secinu: Sangrija.
Pirmais ērms saka: ja darbā nav jābūt, ja iedzert jums gribas, ja tērzēt vajag par lietiņām senām, tad nāciet mums līdzi, mums baznīcas ēzē vēl daudz tādu pudeļu, lūk, ņemiet šis slēpes, lūk, velciet šos aizkarus.
Mēs cēlamies, mūrīti atstājām vienu, sniegā palika *tagad* un pudele. Mēs četratā nozudām baznīcas sānā.

MILTI UN SĀLS

Par spīti apkaimes šefpavāru koleģiālajiem pūliņiem un parasto iedzīvotāju laipnajiem aicinājumiem pārtraukt šo neprātu, tādi savas lietas entuziasti kā abi Felipes un Džanluidži turpināja meklēt spageti, pennes un papardelle iežus Po upes baseina atradnēs.

Kāda gan nelaime piemeklējusi nabaga vīrus – sprieda ļaudis mazajos apkaimes krodziņos, vērdamies kā melnacainas meitenes miecēja un stīdzināja pastu – paskatieties uz viņu sejām – ļaudis, malkodami saldu vīnu, kreņķējās – kas ir tā izteiksme? – un šmauga lombardiete tumšos svārkos pienesa vīriem ar spinātiem olīveļļā aizdarītas čiabatas un sausiņus, ko vīnā… – un acis! acis! kā stikla nūdeles – un jauna daiļava pasniedzās pēc šķēlītes vītinātas gaļas – viņiem nav gribas vairāk nemaz – ieminējās maigas māmiņas svārkos ieķēries puišelis – tā ir, dēls, šos vīrus ir pārmācis tas, kas dzen tevi pretim ananāsiem, papaijām un fizāļiem, bet ietriec miltos un sālī – un piemīlīgi slaika meiča nolika uz galda vēl sierus, vēl riekstus

* * *

Nav grūti nokļūt jebkurā pasaules malā,
Pieiet pie ūdens – skatīties, skatīties, peldēt.

Uz silta akmens sēžot, toreiz tev teicu –
Ūdens ir muskulis.

Muskulis saraujas vienmēr, kad tu peldi.

The other freak then asks: but what does that ancient word mean.
It, says I, has meanings more than its share, it turns off time and braids everyday life in a string but basically the meaning is *now*.
Yet again the freak keeps at it: don't you guys have to work?
We go, both of us: no.
Hearing that, the freak hands me the bottle. No more than a fifth left. I empty the blown glass vessel in one mouthful and conclude: Sangria.
The first freak then says: if you don't have to go to work, if you would like a drink, if you need to talk about things ancient and bygone, then come with us, we have many such bottles left in the church hearth, get on these 'ere skis, put on these curtains.
We got up leaving the low wall alone, *now* remained in the snow along with the bottle. The four of us vanished through the side of the church.

FLOUR AND SALT

Despite the combined efforts of the local chefs and sincere pleas of the ordinary folk to put an end to this madness, such enthusiasts as the two Felippes and Gianluigi continued to search for spaghetti, penne, and pappardelle deposits in the Po riverbed.

What misfortune has struck the poor guys – people worried in the little local tavernas, looking at dark-eyed girls tanning and sprouting pasta – look at their faces – sipping their sweet wine, people fretted – what is that expression? –and a lithe Lombardian in a dark skirt brought the men ciabattas sprinkled with olive oil and crackers for the wine… – and these eyes! these eyes! like glass noodles – and a young beauty reached for a slice of air-dried meat – they no longer have any will – ventured a little boy tugging at his mummy's skirt – that's true son, these men are obsessed with what drives you toward pineapples, papayas and groundcherries, yet propels you into flour and salt – and an attractively slender girl put on the table more cheese, more nuts.

* * *

It is not difficult to get to any place in the world,
Walk up to the water – stare, stare, then swim.

Sitting on a warm rock that time I told you:
Water is a muscle.

Water contracts every time you swim.

MĀRIS SALĒJS

PHOTO: RAIMONDS BRIEDIS

MĀRIS SALĒJS (real name Marians Rižijs) was born in 1971 in Riga. A poet, artist, and scholar, Salējs published his first collection of poetry and translations from Polish *Māmiņ es redzēju dziesmu* (Mummy I Saw a Song / Riga: Enigma) in 1999. His second, award winning collection, *Mana politika* (My Politics / Riga: Pētergailis), followed in 2001 to general acclaim.

A prolific book reviewer, Salējs is also the author of scholarly analyses of the poetry of such living Latvian classics as Uldis Bērziņš, Jānis Rokpelnis, and Knuts Skujenieks. The poems in the following selection are from his third, hitherto unpublished collection.

No cikla 'Privātais alfabēts. Zibšņi'

* * *

A.

a burts ir skaists. burts a ir kā apaļa acs
burts a mirdz lapotnē. burts a skatās manī
nemirkšķēdams iz aliču biežņas pie ūdensbākas.
burts a nāk no pirmajiem gadiem.
viņš redz dzeltenu sienu un vietu kur
bija reiz suns. Suns ir nomiris un būda norakta.
tur tagad ūdensbāka. Pilna ar smagu
mirdzošu ūdeni ko piedzīvojušas visādas
sīkbūtnes. Vēl ilgi varētu skatīties atspulgā
sviest tajā pārkniebtus tūju čiekurus kam
balzama smarža. tad pa ūdens
virsu izlīst varavīkšņaini loki.
saceļas vējš un kāds sauc pusdienās.
uz virtuvi. es redzu vecomāti
kas no pavārnīcas lej kaut ko zeltainu.
sauli. ēnu. diļļu smaržu. truša gabalu. zivi

paņem maizīti viņa saka

nē noskaitīsim lūgšanu

(caur mušu dūkšanu)

tā labi

* * *

ak tāda ir tā pāriešana no vienas puses otrā
tik viegla tik nemanāma
kā piliena tinkšķis pret ūdens vāku
ūdensmērītāju burzmā
pavisam tuvu viņu pirkstgaliem
ūdensdzirkstelēm aizskrienot pār atspulgiem

tik palsi skanot

From the series 'Private Alphabet. Flashes'

* * *

A.

the letter a is beautiful. the letter a is like an apple of the eye
the letter a radiates from the foliage. the letter a stares at me
unblinking from the jungle of Caucasian plums by the water barrel.
the letter a comes from the first years.
he sees a yellow wall and the place where
once there was a dog. The dog has died and the doghouse is buried.
that's where the water barrel is now. Full of heavy
radiant water crowded with all kinds of
infinitesimal life. I could keep staring at the reflection
throw at it broken thuja cones with
their balsamic aroma. then the water
surface is painted over by rainbows.
wind springs up and someone is calling me to lunch.
in the kitchen. I see my grandmother
pouring something golden from the ladle.
the sun. shadow. fragrance of dill. piece of rabbit. fish

get a piece of bread she says

no let's pray

(through the spray of flies)

that's good

* * *

so that's what transition from one side to the other is like
so light so imperceptible
like the tinkle of a droplet against water's lid
in a crowd of water-strides
very close to their toes
as water-sparks scatter over the reflections

resounding opaquely

* * *

caurspīdībai ir savi likumi
es zinu. nāk zvaigzne un sabojā stiklu
tā ir tik tieša. tik vieliska
spiežas cauri un lauskas pa ielu
tad elpu ņem apdzisis gaiss
un dzeltena gaisma pielīst
pilna ar acīm. visu tumsībā stingušo acīm
pielijušiem ar miegu
pielijušiem ar kaut ko neizsakāmu

tā arī nespējušiem saprast: izšķīst
vai savākties biezās dūrēs priekš esmēm

* * *

– do you go to Bethlehem?
are you going?... do you go?
nē... debesī mirdz strīpa
līdz pašām pazarēm

es palieku mierā
mans nams ir celts
no tēstiem baļķiem un durvīs
kliņķis no dzelzs

man tikai jānospiež
kas tur liels?
doties ceļā
kur piedzimst Dievs...

– do you go to Bethlehem?
are you going?...do you go?
– I don't know. maybe...

* * *

transparency has its rules
I know. a star comes and ruins the glass
it is so frank. so material
it pushes through and shards scatter over the street
then an extinguished air takes the breath away
and a yellow light is drenched
full of eyes. eyes of all those frozen in darkness
drenched with sleep
drenched with the unspeakable

proving still unable to resolve: dissolve
or gather in thick fists for being

* * *

– do you go to Bethlehem?
are you going?… do you go?
no… a bright streak in the sky
up to the lower branches

I remain calm
my house is built
of hewn logs and on my door
a handle wrought of iron

I only have to press
what's the big deal?
to depart for
where God is born…

– do you go to Bethlehem?
are you going?… do you go?
– I don't know. maybe…

* * *

attālinās noasiņodama Tava elpa
izšķaidot mākoņus sarkanus tālē

kā gribas kliegt – mans mūžs ir veltīgs
kā siseņi blīgznu zaros

un starpzvaigžņu telpa
vientuļos plaušu galos

* * *

arvienu pareizticīgāk es tevi mīlu
mans ēnu leģions jau kļuvis netīrs
kopš atkusnis liek sniegam spožam
samelnēt. tak retais
mirklis kurā plaukstu tevi redzēt
vēl uztur līdzsvarā šo miesu apjukušo
ar divi kājām staigājot pa ielu
kam slaiki bērzu stumbri abpus

pār melniem viļņiem stāvus zaļas lapas
kā buras paslējušās. labs tas
gaismas aploks noausts aplīk dienai.
ver acis ciet. būs vieglāk saglabāt
mums pirmās pieskaršanās skurbumu
pirms aklas pirmatnības sašķelts gaiss
mums elpas plēsīs neskaitāmās zvaigznēs

* * *

bet manu rociņu tu tomēr neapturi

kluss. vakars saritina buru
un priežu galvas paliek nekustīgas
vējš stāj. beidz pūst. es tevi klusi turu
pie dzīvības. kā trauslu stiklu

kā savu elpu pēdējo

* * *

bleeding your breath draws away
scattering clouds of red in the distance

how I want to scream – I live in vain
like locusts in the branches of willows

and the interstellar space
on the lonely tips of my lungs

* * *

my love for you is growing orthodox
the legion of my shadows dirty
since the thaw made the pure bright snow
turn black. yet the rare
moment in which I bloom to see you
still keeps this baffled flesh in balance
when walking on two feet down the road
with birches slender on both sides

green leaves billow upright over black waves
protruding like ship's sails. it's good
the fence of light that's woven round the day.
close your eyes for it will be easier to keep
the elation of our virgin touching
before the air split by primeval blindness
shreds our breaths in countless stars

* * *

well please don't stop my little hand

it's quiet. evening furls its sails
and heads of pines are keeping still
the wind dies down. stops blowing. I keep you quietly
alive. like fragile glass.

like my breath. my very last

* * *

es zinu – tavs bērns ir jūra
pie tavas ietekas stāvu un skatos
kā tu viņu uzturi
(un arī zivis spurainas
peld viņas asinī sabiezējušā
kas nāk no tavas vienīgās dzīslas

* * *

es skumstu par sevi – ka manis vairs nav
vēl gaisos vasaras vakari stāv
pilni ar straujām čurkstīšu švīkām
un lielceļa putekļu kustībām dīkām

cik žēl ka manis vairs nav
cik žēl ka es nedzirdu vairs
savu elpu pa vidu gaisam

es biju gaidījis kaut ko skaistu

cik skaisti bet manis vairs nav

* * *

pilienos sairis visums. pusnaktī klīstam starp zvaigznēm manīju pilienu pulku. vienā pilienā – putns, otrā – stiebrs. trešajā – dziesma no putna. Ceturtā – mizas gabals ar skudru, kas skrēja uz pūzni. no pūžņa sestajā pilienā – skuja.

Es vairs nezināju, ko tas varēja vēstīt.
tikai jutu, ka naktī uz ceļa ir vēsi.
ceļā uz simtkārt pamesto dzimteni.

* * *

I know your child is the sea
I stand at your mouth and watch
how you take care of it
(and fish with razor fins
swim in its thickened blood
that's flowing from your single vein)

* * *

I grieve for myself – that I am no more
summer evenings still up in the air
full of screeches of fast flying martins
and dust from the road in lazy motion

pity that I am no more
pity I no longer hear
the sound of my breath in midair

I had thought it would be beautiful

how beautiful but I am no more

* * *

the universe dissolved into droplets. at midnight I saw wandering amongst the stars a multitude of droplets. in the first droplet a bird in the second a grass blade. in the third the song of the bird. In the fourth a piece of barkwith an ant scurrying to the anthill. in the sixth droplet from the ant-hill a pine needle.

I no longer knew what the message could be.
just felt that it's chilly at night on the road.
the road to the homeland a hundred times left.

* * *

redzi kas paliek no plēsoņām?
kauli

redzi kas paliek no dzīvības?
saule

kad vienmēr ir cauri
tad atkal šī saule

nezinu kāpēc
bet jā

* * *

kā tumši spārni abpus pletās mežs
pa ceļa balto mugurkaulu braucām
jau zaudējuši dvēseles. vējš sniega putekļus
un kauca

tad austrums atmirdzēja spožos plankumos
un apsolīja brīdi neizdzist

par cilvēku uz brīdi palicis
tam stiklā atspīdēju tāls un svešs

* * *

te nu mēs esam

nāve nesedz mūs
pilnīgi

tātad esam

* * *

see what remains of predators?
bones

see what remains of life?
sun

when it is always all over
then again this sun

I don't know why
but is

* * *

like darkened wings the woods spread out
us driving down the bone-white spine of road
our souls already lost. the wind was snowing dust
and howling loud

then the dawn shone forth in brilliant patches
promising to glow a spell

turned for a moment human
I was reflected in its glass a distant stranger

* * *

here we are

death does not cover us
completely

therefore we are

* * *

kāda melna slāpe pēc tevis ak dzīve
svešādā zaļā un mirdzošā
sirdsžēlīgi kā piparmētru
mežs pirms nevainīgas
ieņemšanas ja
tu gribi piemēram šo skaistumu
vēl redzēt zinu nevarēsi vairs
tik dzidri tik atdevīgi
skatīt visu kas te nolikts mirgo
cīruļdziesmu augstu gaisā tuvu
tuvu Dieva spīdeklim un zemāk
rudzu druvu līdz pat zilgai meža malai ar
ceļa stīdziņu kreisajā pusē uz dusu
kā uz dusu nesaprotu kas tā sāp
nepareizi notikušais kā no vāts
izlāsusī esme kāda milzīga
kļūda to saprast kāda šausmīga
kliedziena plaisa pār visu kāds
sastrēdzis visums pie velna
un es un es un es te vēl kā punktēta
līnija ceļa stīdziņā pāri grantij un
bedru peļķu topogrāfijai tik neizprotami
ak Jēzu neizprotami kam
pieder šī saskaldītā elpa kas tā elš
kas viņam lāso

un ko viņš vairs saprot zem
kaistošā augusta saules dzeltenuma

* * *

vārdu pilieni smadzeņu akās saviļņo spoguli
spodrajām jūlija debesīm izliecoties
ap seju kurā nojaust var
vieglas ņirbas kropļotus
bērnības vaibstus

* * *

what dark thirst for you life
strange one green and radiant
heart-merciful like a peppermint
forest before immaculate
conception if
you would like for instance to see
this beauty I know you won't be able any more
to purely yieldingly
take in all that's placed here shining
lark-song there up high so near
to the heavenly body and below
the rye field up to the bluish streak of forest
the tendril of a path to the left to sleep
what sleep I don't understand what hurts so much
what happened wrong like existence
trickled out from a wound what huge
mistake to understand that what horrible
cracking scream over everything
haemorrhaging universe to hell with it
and me and me and me I am still
a dotted line in the tendril path over the gravel
the topography of holes puddles so incomprehensibly
oh Jesus so puzzling to whom
belongs this choppy breath that wheezes so
what drips from him

and what he can comprehend under
this blistering yellow of the August sun

* * *

the droplets of words in brain wells ruffle the mirror
as the bright july sky bends
around a face in which one can read
features of childhood
distorted by rippling light

* * *

laiks. pietiks skumt par tādiem
kādi esam. jā ik pārdien. protams tumst
šī zeme padebešu apvalkā

un nāve traktoriņā apkaltā
ar laukus. nez ko vēlāk sēs?
mirdz blīvas velēnas. ar violeta māla
valgo dvašu izgaro kas bij reiz zvaigznes
nokaitēta acs. jā

skumt vairs nevajag
meži aug kā silts pret ziemu
zvēram kažoks. uzplēsts lauks
tvan savu elpu tālai zvaigznei

bet nāves simetriskais atveids peļķē atviz
kad tā no lauka mājup brauc kad nakts –

* * *

marts. nodreb cilvēki zem pirkstiem
un mostas radītājs no sava snauda

viņš logā redz cik grubuļota gaisma
un zeme detaļās tik smalkās ka top bail

tad aizvien spalgāk saprot: nē
pār mani Augstāks valda. te

ar Viņu strīds kā sīku putnu bars
pa zaru režģi lēkāt ņemas

* * *

miers. no staba aizlido stārks
(nekā labāka nebūs)
koki sakūst par valni
mieži izstaro vasarā iekrāto gaismu

* * *

it's time. enough to grieve over such
as we are. yes year in year out. darkens yes
this land encased by clouds

and death on a tractor loud
is ploughing. what will be sown?
the dense sod aglow. with the damp breath
of purple clay evaporates what once was star's
white-hot eye. Indeed

no need to grieve
forests grow against the winter warm
as fur on beasts. the torn up field
breathes hot for a distant star

but the symmetry of death is mirrored in a puddle
as it drives home from the field when it is night –

* * *

march. people tremble under fingers
and creator wakes from his slumber

he sees how pockmarked is the light
and the earth is in such tiny parts it's scary

then his understanding grows more shrill: no
a Higher One is ruler. here

quarrelling with Him is like a flock of tiny birds
hopping in the grid of branches

* * *

peace. a stork flies off a post
(there will be nothing better)
trees melt into a wall
barley radiates light stored from the summer

mijkrēšļa gaiss staigā caur lapām kas
rudenī birs. ir silts

uz ceļa vēl redzami sabrauktie krupji

* * *

vārnas savos dzejoļos ielaiž
liktenīgas kļūdas. pēc tam
nelaimīgas staigā pa peļķēm
un dzer netīru ūdeni

mazas meitenes viņas ierauga
un priecīgas skrien pakaļ: vārna vārna!
bet viņas bēg neveikli plātot spārnus
un atstājot slapjus pēdu nospiedumus
uz ietves. vēlāk klusi raud
paslēpušās zem mašīnām jo nemāk
rakstīt gramatiski pareizus
dzejoļus

TRĪS DZEJOĻI RYUČĀNA GARĀ

1.

ierauts rudens fiziķiem pārpilnā dienā
tu vēro kā viens no viņiem izvelk gravitācijas
konstanti no slīpi krītošas lapas trajektorijas

cits savukārt palēkdamies diedz pakaļ brūnam
kastanim mērīdams atsitiena spēku pret dzelzbetona
taciņu. laikam rēķina elastības koeficientu –
tu spried pamukdams malā jo tieši tad baltas
dzirksteļu šaltis šķiezdams no pagrieziena iznirst
tramvajs

vadītāja kabīnē visus kloķus rausta
trešais fiziķis. šķiet pēta berzes īpašības…

the twilight air wafts through the leaves that
will fall in autumn. it is warm

the run-over toads still on the road

* * *

crows in their poems make
fatal mistakes. then
they walk through puddles unhappy
drinking foul water

little girls see them
and run after them gleeful: a crow a crow!
but they flee spreading their clumsy wings
leaving wet footprints
on the pavement. later they weep quietly
huddled under cars for they don't know how
to write poems
grammatically correct

THREE POEMS IN THE MANNER OF RYUČĀNS

1.

caught in a day full of fall physicists
you watch as one of them extracts the gravitation
constant from the trajectory of a sideways falling leaf

another one is leaping after a brown
horse chestnut, measuring its rebound force against the concrete
pathway. must be calculating the ratio of flexibility –
you surmise jumping aside for at that moment spraying
white sparks a tram appears from around the
corner

pulling all levers in the driver's cabin
sits the third physicist. seems to be examining the properties of friction…

beidzot tev pielec: viņi visi savākušies šeit
lai novērotu pasaules ainu. kuru katru

brīdi tai jāsagrūst zem dzērvju klaigām spējas smaržas vai
bērnībā dzirdētas mūzikas

tādēļ visi vēdlodziņi tiek spēji aizcirsti
gaisma izdzēsta. faili saspiesti

2.

viens prasa kā iet un smaržo iela kā parasts
šai ziemā pēc sniega kas sabraukts brūns
kā manas bērnības šerbets uz ko
es pamāju atbildei galvu – jā viss
notiek un vakar piemēram ieslēdzis tālrādi
es ļoti brīnījos kad pretī man rēgojās tumsa

tas gan nav labi – tas otrs teica: jo redzi
bērnībā dziļā es redzēju sapni
būdams pavisam trīs gadus mazs: tur
luksofors stāvēja ielas malā
un rādīja sarkanu gaismu kas
izrādījās marmelāde un es tur gandrīz līdz nāvei ieķepu

sīkums – es teicu: tas viss ir sīkums kādā dienā tu redzēsi
ka viss ir galīgi otrādi. piemēram mēs tagad
stāvam daudzus tūkstošus gadus vecā atmiņā un
Viens visai miglaini atceras mūsu vaibstus kādā
pīlādžu čemuriem pilnā ielā

– kādi pīlādži?
– tie lielie
trešā oga no apakšas. tūdaļ nodzisīs

viņš atkāpjas un sniegs nogurkst zem viņa kājām

finally you get it: they have all gathered here
to observe the world situation. any time

now it can collapse under the shrieks of cranes a sudden aroma or
music heard in childhood

that's why all ventilation panes are suddenly slammed shut
lights out files compressed

2.

someone asks how goes it and the street smells as it
normally does this winter of snow that's turned brown under the wheels
like the sherbet I used to have as a child
I nod in reply – yes things
are happening for instance yesterday when I turned on the TV
I was surprised to see darkness staring at me

that's no good – the other one said: 'cause see
in early childhood I had a dream
I was just all of three: there
was a traffic light at the corner
and it had on the red light which
turned out to be marmalade and I almost got stuck there and died

no big deal – I said: none of it is a big deal one day you'll see
that it's the other way round. we for example now
stand in memory many thousands of years old and
Someone is barely remembering our features in some
street of rowan berries

– what rowan?
– those big ones
the third berry from the bottom. it's about to go out

he steps back and the snow crackles under his feet

3.

mīļai piemiņai no 1999. gada 11. augusta saules aptumšošanās

pēc tam no tumsas iznirst hologrāfisks vasaras attēls
ar visiem tauriņiem acu augstumā stingušiem
snuķīšu stiebriem tiecoties uz kaut kādiem dzelte
niem ziedvidiem dzīslotu kātu galos

tā kā jāsmaržo būtu bet gaiss laikam iestrē
dzis molekulu konfigurācijās nevar pasmaržot

ēna uz taciņas tas laikam ezis cik savādi
spurains kāpēc pa dienu kaut
kas te neģeld šajā bildē
nav lāga

ā rekur rakstīts: dubultekspo
zīcija ar zariņu smiltīs un
saules sirpis pār mežu

* * *

labi. mēs finansēsim jūsu skumjas
bet tām jābūt īpaši mēļām
apmēram kā tā pamale pie apvāršņa
redzat? tur kur bērzu birzs aizsedz
sīciņo egļu strēli

un ja ķirši zaros ir gluži vai melni
arī tas tiks ieskaitīts mūsu bilancē
jo katra intensitāte atpelnīsies ar uzviju

ceļa šķēlums gan visu dara gaisīgu
baltu putekļu blīva aizsedz skatienam aizbraucējus

bet arī tas saskaņots. vieglums
kuru mums nepārmākt. skumjas
kā drīksna liegajā visuma ziedā

3.

in loving memory of the solar eclipse 11 August 1999

then a holographic image of summer emerges from the dark
complete with butterflies frozen at eye-level
their stem-like proboscis reaching for some yel
low mid-flowers topping nervate stems

should be some aroma but the air must be mir
ing in some configurations of molecules
failing its fragrance

a shadow on the pathway I guess it's a hedgehog how strangely
prickly why in the daytime some
thing wrong with this picture
not right

oh see the inscription: double expo
sure with a twig in the sand and
crescent sun over the woods

* * *

all right. we will finance your sorrow
only make sure it is purple enough
like that sky by the horizon
see? where the birch grove blocks the view to
the tiny growth of pine

and if the cherries on the tree are almost black
that will appear on our balance sheet
for any intensity earns interest

the fork in the road makes it all ephemeral true
the white cloud of dust covers those that leave

but that too has been agreed. lightness
we cannot suppress. sorrow
a stigma in the gentle bud of universe

* * *

lūk tur aizpeld manas valsts miniatūrie mērogi
pāri gigantiskajām paēnām.
no atskurbtuves izlaiž mēnesi

lēnām
tikko atmodies viņš rāpaļā augšup
viegla paģiru nimba ieskauts

bet zeme nemitīgi tam atgādina
par sudrabaino pienākumu. koks klana
galvu līdzi. jā jā jā. būkšķ kastaņi

no centrālstacijas aug dūmi
tur aizvēsturieksie vilcieni
ar svilpieniem sasaucas
skalodami savos tvaika katlos
uzkarsētu miglas šķidrumu

dūmi kāpj vējos
dūmi no pilsētas ielejas ceļas uz putnu ceļu

tur cielavas
citi mazi erickiņi
zeltgalvīši cierē uz dienvidiem

un sirds jau arī raujas viņiem līdzi
sīkās zemes līdziniece

* * *

vasaras krāsainais punktiņš atmiņās deg visu ceļu
paceļu galvu – tumsti: dzirkstelēm piesētā elle

pieslēdzas lakstīgala strāvai no rožu krūma
staigāju pasaules malu. nezinu. ko vairs runāt

palikšu tavai skaņai. sienāžu pilnai zālei
palikšu. tad jau manīs. sairt liesmās vai bālēt

* * *

see the miniature of my country float away
over the gigantic shades
moon is let out from the drunk tank

slowly
just awakened he scrambles up
light hangover wrapped halo-like around him

yet the earth keeps reminding him
of his silvery duty. the tree keeps
nodding along. yes yes yes thud the chestnuts

smoke blooms from the central station
prehistoric trains
converse with whistles
swishing in their steam cauldrons
fog's scalding liquid

the smoke climbs in the wind
the wind climbs from the vale of the city to the bird routes

where the wagtails
and other tiny upstarts
goldcrests trek southward

and the heart keeps yearning to go along
that twin of this here tiny land

* * *

the colourful dot that is summer burns in memory all the way
I lift my head – dark: the hell strewn full of sparks

the nightingale plugs in from the rose bush
I walk on the far side of the world. don't know. what to say.

I will stay for your sound. grass teeming with grasshoppers.
I will stay. then we'll see. to fall apart in flames or to fade.

KĀRLIS VĒRDIŅŠ

PHOTO: JĀNIS INDĀNS

Kārlis Vērdiņš was born in 1979 in Riga. With an M.A. in Cultural Theory and a Ph.D. in Philology, Vērdiņš is the author of many academic papers (including a book on prose poetry, *Bastarda forma*, (2010)) and essays on literature, both Latvian and foreign, as well as a prolific literary critic. He has published four volumes of poetry *Ledlauži* (Icebreakers / Riga: Nordic, 2001, 2nd ed. 2009), *Biezpiens ar krējumu* (Cottage Cheese with Sour Cream / Riga: Atēna, 2004), *Burtiņu zupa* (Alphabet Soup, for children, 2007), and *Es* (I / Riga: Neputns, 2008), all to a great critical and popular acclaim and fetching top literary awards. Vērdiņš has also written librettos and song lyrics and has published translations of American Modernist poetry (T. S. Eliot, W. C. Williams, H.D., *et al*). His own poetry has been translated in many languages, including collections in Russian and Polish.

COME TO ME

Es tev vedu mazu siermaizīti. Bija jau divi naktī, visi kļuvuši miegaini, veikali ciet, bet bārā "*I love you*" es dabūju mazu siermaizīti.

Braucu ar taksi un vedu tev siermaizīti, jo tu gulēji bēdīgs, varbūt pat slims, un mājās nebija nekā garšīga. Briesmīgi dārga, kaut kur ap latu, bet tas nekas.

Braucu ar savu mazo *ailavjū*, saspiestu, gandrīz jau atdzisušu. Bet sanāca tā, ka neaizbraucu uz mājām. Nokļuvu tur, kur visi līksmi un asprātīgi, un ļoti izsalkuši. Iedzēru, uzdziedāju, bet maizīti pataupīju.

Laikam tikai trešajā dienā beidzot varēju tevi pacienāt, tu biji tik nikns, ka apēdi maizīti, lāgā to neapskatījis. Būtu es drosmīgāks, būtu teicis – tu taču zini, ka es tevi mīlu, tu taču zini, ka apbrīnoju. Neliec man, lai atkal to saku.

DHARMAS LAUKĀ

Mēs te sēžam un ēdam kartupeļus, bet Rembo un Verlēns jau ir Briselē. Esot uzrakstījuši daudz jaunu dzejoļu.

Mēs te Lielajos kapos dzeram alu, izglītojam cits citu un paši paliekam galīgi skābi. Bērns raud celiņa malā.

Ardžuna sacīja: "Man nevajag ne karaļvalsts, ne laimes, tikai vēl vienu dienu nesēdēt pie tā smirdīgā datora." Un saļima viņš pie kāda pelēka kapakmens.

Kuš, lasi tālāk! Viņi esot jau Londonā! Visapkārt esot dzeltena migla. Bet mums bambuks aug griezdamies vāzītē virtuvē.

Londonas spiegu ziņojumus jau aplūko Briseles datoros. Bet mums te virtuvē zilā bļodiņā sīpols. Izkurtējis, atdevis visu spēku zaļam lociņu pušķītim.

ĒRGLIM

Patiešām, no augšas viss izskatās citādi – ja nav mākoņu, varam saredzēt ļaudis, kas lejā kustas kā skudras, un viņu slepenos priekus, sadzirdēt biklās lūgšanas, kuras šeit iegrāmato un pieņem zināšanai tavi mazākie kolēģi plikiem, apaļiem vēderiem.

COME TO ME

I was bringing you a little cheese sandwich. It was two in the morning, everybody sleepy, shops closed but in the *I Love You* bar they gave me a little cheese sandwich.

I was in a taxi bringing you a little cheese sandwich 'cause you were lying there sad, perhaps even ill, and there was nothing good to eat in the house. Was real expensive, around one lat, but that's OK.

So I was in the taxi with my little *iluvu*, all squished, practically cold. But for some reason I didn't make it home. Somehow I ended up where all were merry and witty, and starving. So I drank, I sang, but I saved my little sandwich.

Must have been the third day when I could finally treat you to it, you were so angry, you ate the sandwich hardly looking at it. Had I had more courage, I would have said: but you know I love you, you know I admire you. Don't make me say it again.

IN THE DHARMA FIELD

We sit here eating potatoes, whereas Rimbaud and Verlaine have long since gone to Brussels. They say they've written many new poems.

We sit here in the Great Cemetery drinking beer, educating one another and turning really sour ourselves. There's a child crying by the side of the path.

Said Arjuna: "I have no need for a kingdom or happiness, just one more day away from that stinking computer." And he collapsed by some grey headstone.

Shush, go on reading! They say they are already in London! Yellow fog all around. Whereas we have a shoot of bamboo thriving in a vase in the kitchen.

Spy messages from London are already examined on Brussels computers. Whereas we have an onion in a blue bowl in the kitchen. All withered, given its strength to a green clump of sprouts.

TO THE EAGLE

Indeed from above it all looks different – it there are no clouds, we can see people scurrying down below like ants, can see their secret pleasures, hear their shy prayers which here are filed away and noted by your smaller colleagues with naked, round bellies.

Viņi apskauž tevi un nemīl, apvainojas, kad izdzird starp mākoņiem tavus pērkondimdošos smieklus. Tava bārda viegli noplīv pār viņiem, un tu atkal aizlido tālāk uz kādu dievu pamestu kaktu izgulēt reibumu krēslainā zileņu cērpā.
Es pie izlietnes mazgāju glāzes, klausos viņu balsteļu murdoņā, klusītēm smaidu – es vienīgais zinu, kur tu pazūdi pusdienas vidū, aizveru acis – es vienīgais zinu, kur tu atnāksi šonakt.
Citkārt man ļauts vien slepus pieskarties tavam plecam, kad apkalpoju pie garā galda, kur jūs baudāt sarkanbaltsarkanus vīnus.
Es biju valdnieks pār dumjām aitām, bet tāšu kronis palika pļavā, kad ērglis, mani sagrābis, pacēla gaisā. Kad krūtīs pirmoreiz iedūrās viņa asais un maigais knābis.

EŅĢELIS

"Are you my Angel?"
Allen Ginsberg, *A Supermarket in California*

Jā, es esmu tavs eņģelis, šovakar izdzīts no debesīm ietīt tev celofānā gurušu, vītušu ābolīti, kuru tik daudzreiz vienas kāras rokas devušas otrām. Izpārdošana šonakt: zaļi augļi – ar atlaidēm, mirusi miesa – uz nomaksu.
Neteic nevienam, es esmu tavs eņģelis, Mikelandželo izdreijāts Dāvids; ja šonakt skūpstītu manas plaukstas, dzinkstētu pirkstu kauliņu porcelāns; "Tavas debesis acu krāsā", sēktu ausī, jo esi dzejnieks.
Nez, cik tu dabūtu, izjaucis mani un detaļās pārdevis patiltes utenī? Pudeli džina, ko viebjoties tukšot ar upeņu zapti miroņiem pilnas istabas krēslā, kopā ar svešu veci no bāra; viņš apreibis muldēs par tankiem, promejot nozags tev naudas maku.
Šonakt aiz katras letes pa eņģelim, vai nav tiesa, ikviens smaida platāk, nekā darba līgumā pieprasīts; maiņa beidzas, tie, savicinājuši spārniņus, aiztrauc uz pustukšām istabiņām ar kailu spuldzi un krāsni kaktā, kur vēsās rokas saņems un nomutēs kādu mīļu un sprogainu galvu.
Kungs aiz tevis jau skaita naudu. Varbūt visas plūmes un banānus, varbūt visu lieltirgotavu viņš nopirks, un mani piedevām; noliks plauktā aiz stiklotām durvīm, bieži slaucīs ar astru slotiņu, debesis pulēs ar plīša strēmeli.
Neklaigā, neplāties. Žigli izvelc no kabatām gurķus, palūdz, lai tevi aizved uz mājām; neskumsti, uzraksti dzejolīti.

They envy you and do not love you, they take offence, hearing through the clouds your thundering laughter. Your beard lightly brushes past them and you fly off to some god forsaken corner to sleep off drunkenness in some bilberry bush.
I wash glasses by the sink, listen to the murmur of their voices and smile to myself – I alone know where you disappear in the middle of the day, I close my eyes – I alone know where you will appear tonight.
At other times I am allowed to barely touch your shoulder when I serve at the long table where you drink red-white-red wines.
I reigned over dumb sheep, yet my crown of birch bark was left in the meadow when the eagle grabbed me and lifted me up. When his sharp and gentle beak first pierced my chest.

ANGEL

"Are you my Angel?"
Allen Ginsberg, *A Supermarket in California*

Yes, I am your angel, driven out of heaven tonight to wrap a wary wilted apple for you, an apple passed so many times from one pair of greedy hands to another. Sale tonight: green fruit at a discount, dead flesh by instalment.

Don't tell anyone, I am your angel, David shaped by Michelangelo; if my hands were kissed tonight, their knuckle porcelain would tinkle; "Your sky is the colour of eyes", ever the poet, you'd wheeze.
I wonder how much you'd get selling my parts at the flea market? A bottle of gin mixed with jam and drunk wincing in a dimly-lit room full of dead bodies, shared with a stranger picked up at a bar; boozy, he'd babble of tanks, upon leaving he'd snatch your wallet.
An angel behind every counter tonight, aren't their smiles broader, than the contract requires; the shift is over, in a flutter of wings, they take off to their half-empty rooms: a naked bulb, a stove in the corner, cool cradling hands, a kiss on that sweet, curly-haired head.
The gent behind you is busy counting his money. He'll buy all the plums and bananas, he'll buy the supermarket perhaps, and I'll be included; he'll set me on a shelf behind glass, dust me off with a horsehair brush, polish heaven with a strip of plush.
Stop shouting, stop bragging. Quick, take the cucumbers out of your pockets, request to be taken home; don't fret, write a poem.

ES

Ja es kontrolēju savu iekšējo orgānu darbību, tad tas vēl nenozīmē, ka man tādu vispār nav. Joprojām aknas, plaušas un nieres riņķo ap manu sirdi, zvēro un deg.

Daudz mazu zvaigžņu pukst manī dzalkstīdamas, šūpojas, krīt. Un tad es palieku slims. Istabā lēni mainās gaisma un tumsa. Jūtu – daudz mazu pilsētu riņķo ap Rīgu spiegdamas, drebinādamās salā.

Ik mirkli es zaudēju milzīgu daudzumu enerģijas un siltuma. Tāpēc gribu, lai tu lēzenos lokos riņķo ap mani

GANIŅŠ

Tagad man pieder vienīgi paplāte, uz kuras dieviem iznēsāt alkoholu, kad viņi strīdas, viens otru ievaino, sūc tumšo ķekaru lipīgo saldumu.
Katrs aizmieg sarkanā mākonī, apžilbis varenībā un gudrībā. Tad es izdzeru viņu vīnu, bet zemi sagrābj rītausmas rožainie nagi.

IEKŠĒJĀS KĀRTĪBAS NOTEIKUMI

Es neko pretī nerunāju, paskatījos un paklusēju, nopūtos, sēdos pie sava galda. Arī citiem neko daudz neteicu, tikai dažiem pastāstīju, ko es pats par to domāju.
Man taču neviens neprasīja, visu pa kluso izdarīja, un pēc tam nekā mainīt nevarēja.
Tikai vēlāk dzirdēju, kāds esot teicis, ka turpmāk gan būšot citādi – visu jau iepriekš pateikšot, dažiem pat priekšā parādīšot, un savā starpā neko nedrīkstēs runāt, un, pasarg Dies, kaut ko stāstīt uz ārpusi. Tā arī citiem pastāstīju, un kāds bij tik stulbs un gāja prasīt, vai tiešām tā būšot.
Tagad uz mums visi ir ļoti dusmīgi, teica, būs nepatikšanas. Tas mani drusku apbēdināja, bet es to neteicu skaļi. Tikai sēdēju mūsu telpā pie sava galda, tad ienāca viņa, pārlaida acis istabai un aizejot noteica: „Te jau neviena nav”.

I

If I can control the functioning of my inner organs, it does not mean I don't have any. Liver, lungs, and kidneys keep circling around my heart, they smoulder and burn.

Many a little star pulses in me sparking, swaying, and falling. And then I get sick. Light and dark slowly change in the room. I feel this – there are many little cities circling around Riga shrieking, shivering with cold.

Every passing minute I lose huge amounts of energy and warmth. That's why I want you to circle around me slowly.

SHEPHERD

Now I possess but this tray to carry alcohol for the gods, as they quarrel, injure each other, sip the cloying sweetness of the dark grape.

Every one falls asleep in a red cloud, dazzled by his own power and wisdom. Then I drink their wine, and the earth is seized by the rosy talons of dawn.

RULES OF CONDUCT

I did not talk back, just looked and kept quiet, sighed and sat down at my desk. Nor did I say much to the others, except telling some what I think of it all.

Nobody asked me a thing, just went about it quietly and then nothing could be done about it really.

Only later I heard someone had said this would change in the future: everything would be laid out in advance, some would even be shown the ropes, just under no circumstances could it all be discussed and, God forbid, if anything were said to an outsider. That's what I told the others, but someone was stupid enough to go and ask if that would really be the case.

Now everyone is very angry with us, said we were in trouble. That upset me a bit but I wouldn't say it out loud. Just sat in our room by my desk and then she came in, looked around the room and said, upon leaving: "But there is no one here."

JAUNĀ DZĪVE

Sāksim jaunu dzīvi uz vientuļas betona salas ar elektrības stabu un dažām vārnām uz vadiem. Kā divi noguruši ledlauži ielauztiem dibeniem gulēsim liedagā blakus tukšajām alus pudelēm.
Tikai reizēm jāpastiepjas un jānocērt rokas, kas sniedzas pret mums no grimstošiem kuģiem, jāattin kāda pudelē atpeldējusi zīmīte, pēdējie sveicieni sievai un bērniem ar šaušalīgām pareizrakstības kļūdām.
Taču no izmestajām mantām nekā daudz nenoderēs – naktīs, kad alū slīkstošā sala griežas uz riņķi, no tās tiek noskalots viss, kas nav pienaglots, piesiets un iepinies jūraszālēs.
Paliekam vidū apķērušies, kopā savītiem dūmeņiem, laizām tos kā priecīgi pūdeļi. Katra buča pārvērtīsies neaizmirstulītē salas apķēzītajā krastā un astoņos rītā dziedās sirēnas balsī. Un tad mēs iesim uz darbu.

KO TUR LIEGTIES

Es jau teicu, ka esmu noguris – šodien izvilku zebru no degošiem brikšņiem un iecēlu furgonā vienpadsmit saindējušos pingvīnus. Algu neprasu, publicitāti nevajag, tikai mazliet miera un klusuma.

Bet tikmēr posts un aukstums iezadzies manā mājā, kur šie aizjūras darījumi nevienam nav saprotami, un priekšā stāvēja sāpīga izskaidrošanās.

Vai varat iedomāties, daži tiešām jauki un mīļi cilvēki bija vairākas dienas sēdējuši bez ūdens, elektrības un seksa, un neviens nebija varējis viņiem paskaidrot lietas būtību.

Bija vien pašam šī putra jāizstrebj. Gribēju jums to pastāstīt, lai zināt, kādas lietas no manis var sagaidīt.

Bet citādi uzvedos labi, visiem palīdzu, pasauli glābju no sliktajiem zirnekļiem, mācos neeksistēt brīžos, kad tas nav nepieciešams. Pat lietū un slapjdraņķī lidoju pāri pilsētas tumšajām ielām, mans sarkanais apmetnis galīgi netīrs un samircis.

NEW LIFE

We'll start a new life on a solitary concrete island with a power line and a few crows on the wire. Like two tired icebreakers with banged up bottoms we will lie on the beach next to empty beer bottles.
Only once in a while we have to lean over and chop off the hands that try to reach us from sinking ships, unfold a note washed over inside a bottle, the last greetings to wife and kids with horrendous spelling.
Nothing much will come in handy from the things thrown overboard – at night, when the island drowning in beer is turning round and round, everything not nailed down, tied up or stuck in seaweed is washed off.
We remain in the middle, our smokestacks in an embrace, we lick at them like happy poodles. Every kiss will turn into a forget-me-not on the filthy island coast, and will sing like a siren at eight in the morning. And then we will go to work.

WHY DENY IT

Didn't I say already, I'm tired: today I pulled a zebra out of burning bramble and lifted eleven penguins with food poisoning into the trailer. I don't ask to be paid, I need no publicity, just give me some peace and quiet.
Yet meanwhile cold and misery had crept into my house where no body understood these overseas transactions and I had a lot of explaining ahead of me.
Imagine this: some really sweet and nice people had been sitting for several days without water, electricity and sex and no one had been able to explain the heart of the matter to them.
So I had to take care of this mess myself. I just wanted to tell you so you'd know what can be expected of me.
But other than that I am good, ready to help anyone, ready to save the world from the bad spiders; I learn not to exist at moments when it's not necessary. I fly over the dark streets of the city even when it's cold and rainy and my red cloak is all dirty and wet.

LAIKA ZIŅAS

Mākoņus vienmuļā debesī var iekopēt arī no cita negatīva. Šim nolūkam tirdzniecībā dabūjami mākoņu negatīvi, kurus saprātīgi lietojot, var dabūt košu iespaidu.

Mārtiņš Buclers, *Fotogrāfiska ābece* (1905)

Diktors Braiss agri no rīta rakņājas mākoņos, stumda tos uz Meksikas līča pusi un pierunā: „Cienot jūsu vēsturi un tradīcijas, mēs tomēr esam vienojušies atbalstīt patīkamāku laika apstākļu projektus."
Pilnībā kontrolē debesis. Pats tikko pamodināts, gluži silts.
Mākoņi paklausa nelabprāt – vazājas saskrāpētajās debesīs kā lieli, netīri vīrusi, kurina savstarpēju negaisu, spiežas ap diktoru Braisu.
Visas studijas sienas tiek filmētas. Tad, kad beigušās finanšu ziņas, es redzu, kā sudrabains mākonis iesit Braisam, kā viņš krīt, atsizdamies perlamutra mākonī, lido, ķerdamies spalvās un gubās, līdz pazūd apakšā putekļu mākonī.
Miljoniem skatītāju visā pasaulē redz, kā vairāki melnīgsnēji mākoņi demonstratīvi nolīst. Atlikušie peld vairāku jūdžu augstumā, un sākas kultūras ziņas

LIETUS

Vairs nenāk sniegs, bet atnācis lietus. Tu staigā pa savu lielo māju, aizver logus un izslēdz gaismas – rāmā jūgenda paradīzē, kur neiekļūst asas smakas un trokšņi.
Bet lietus – pēkšņs, ass šļāciens – laužas pie tevis caur drošo jumtu un vairākiem stāviem. Tev pieskaras mikla elpa, un nočab papīru kaudzes istabas kaktos.
Pārsteigts un kails tu nometies ceļos, lai lietus tev pātago vaigus un atstāj uz krūtīm karstas lāses.
Bet debesīs atkal kāds nobīstas un aizver ciet rāvējslēdzēju. Tu paliec smacīgā sausumā, mazā valstī, kur cilvēki brīvdienās salien parketa šķirbās un sazin kur pazūd, tavu vārdu izrunāt nemāk un nemāk pareizi uzrakstīt.
Viens tu aizmiedz mijkrēslī lielajā gultā, aizvilcis logam baltus aizkarus. Ārā pumpuri pampst, skrituļi knikšķ, un izpārdošanā tava siltā ziemas jaka maksā vien pusi no puscenas.

WEATHER FORECAST

> *Clouds can be copied onto a solid sky from another negative. Cloud negatives can be bought for this purpose and, when used prudently, can produce a striking image.*
>
> Mārtiņš Buclers, *ABC of Photography (1905)*

Weatherman Brice rises early, rummages through the clouds, pushes them in the direction of the Gulf of Mexico cajoling: "While we respect your history and traditions, we still have agreed to lend support to projects for more agreeable weather patterns."

Has total control over the sky. Having just been awakened himself, still warm with sleep.

The clouds obey but reluctantly – they wander the scratched up sky like large, dirty viruses, they incite mutually assured thunderstorms, they crowd around Weatherman Brice.

All the walls of the studio are being filmed. Once the financial news is over, I see a silvery cloud take a swing at Brice, he tumbles, hitting a mother-of-pearl cloud, flies about and is caught in cirrus and cumuli, then finally disappears in a cloud of dust.

Millions of viewers around the world see how several swarthy clouds demonstratively pour with rain. The remaining just float several miles above ground, and the culture news is now on.

RAIN

No more snow, but rain has come. You walk through your big house, close the windows, and turn off lights – in this quiet art nouveau paradise that keeps pungent odours and noises at bay.

But the rain – a sudden, sharp downpour – is trying to break through to you through the reliable roof and several floors. A damp breath reaches you, stacks of paper rustling in the corners.

Surprised and naked, you fall to your knees, for the rain to lash at your cheeks and cover your chest with hot traces.

But someone gets scared up in the sky and pulls up the zipper. You remain in a dry, stifling place, a small country, where on weekends people crawl into cracks in the parquet disappearing God only knows where, unable to spell your name right or even pronounce it.

Alone, you fall asleep in the big bed in the twilight, white curtains tightly drawn shut. Outside your window buds are swelling, rollers are rambling your warm winter jacket is on sale for half of the half-price.

LIVE

ir tādi koncerta apmeklētāji
kas atpazīst dziesmu pēc pirmajiem ģitāras akordiem
UN TAD VIŅI KLIEDZ

ir tādi apmeklētāji
kas atpazīst pirmā pantiņa sākumu
UN TAD VIŅI KLIEDZ

ir tādi
kas atpazīst tikai piedziedājumu
pēc ceturtās reizes
UN TAD VIŅI KLIEDZ

un vēl ir tādi
kas neatpazīst neko
akli un kurli tie kaktiņā vemj
līdz apsargi viņus iznes no zāles
UN TAD VIŅI KLIEDZ

MĀMIŅ, MAN IR PLĀNS!

Atgriezties atkal dzīvot pie mammas – atbraukt ar visām mantām, godīgi pateikt: māmiņ, es centos, tu pati redzēji, centos. Bet tas viss tomēr nav priekš manis.

Tad varētu gulēt pofigā visu dienu, skatīties seriālus, pārtikt no mammas algas un vēlāk – pensijas. Līdz tam laikam pensijas noteikti jau būs normālas. Palīdzēt viņai nest produktu somu, ļaut, lai sabar, pamāca, apmīļo. Krēslainos ziemas vakaros činkstēt un dīkt:

„Māmiņ, manā vērtību sistēmā nav vieta vīrišķības kategorijai! Māmiņ, savu identitāti es konstruēt gribu kā apzināti marginalizējusies personība! Māmiņ, mana taktika ir visdeviantākais no visiem pašdestrukcijas modeļiem!"

Māmiņa tikai skatītos, smaidītu, domātu: „Gan dēliņš tiks pāri šai nesakarīgajai vervelēšanai un izaugs par jauku sarunu biedru."

LIVE

There are concert goers
who recognize a song by the first chords on the guitar
AND THEN THEY SCREAM

there are goers
who recognize the beginning of the first verse
AND THEN THEY SCREAM

there are
those who recognize only the refrain
after the fourth time
AND THEN THEY SCREAM

and there are those
who don't recognize a thing
blind and deaf they throw up in the corner
until the guards carry them out
AND THEN THEY SCREAM

MUMMY, I HAVE A PLAN!

To go back and live with my mum – to go with all of my things and honestly state: mummy, I tried, you saw for yourself, I really tried. But it simply isn't for me.

Then I could stay in bed all day, watch soap operas, live on mum's salary and later her pension. By that time pensions are sure to be normal. Help her carry the groceries, let her scold me, teach me, hug me. On dark winter evenings keep whining and wailing:

"Mum, in my system of values there is no place for the category of manliness! Mum, I want to construct my identity as a consciously marginalized personality! Mum, my tactic is the most deviant of all the models of self-destruction!"

Mummy would just look and smile, and think: "A time will come when my son gets over this senseless babbling and grows up to be a nice conversation partner."

MĒS

1.

Mēs nedusmojamies uz saviem senčiem,
kas, mīkstos maisos atspieduši saldos rožābolu dupšus,
rātni plūcot zāli, veras ekrānā.
Mēs Jāņu naktī skumji sēžam mājās
un aizmigt nevaram, kad apkārt spiedz un šauj.

2.

Mēs siltumā un gaismā pārziemosim,
sev mājās krāsim asus, trauslus priekšmetus.
Bez ašiem pagriezieniem, straujām kustībām
mēs mīkstā tumsā ieslīdam viens otrā,
lai rītā mostos staru lauskām pilnā gultā.

3.

Mēs dzīvojam bez aizspriedumiem – vari precēt
šo ķirzaku, kas smiltīs gozējas starp sīkiem krūmiem.
Bet atceries – tam pūrā līdz nāks visas vecās astes,
uz plauktiem plastikāta maisos stāvēs jūsu mājā,
bet apakšbikšu kabatiņā pukstēs viņa sirds.

4.

Pie dzīvības un labas veselības
mūs uztur pieklājīgas sarunas ar mīļiem svētku vēlējumiem:
„Ceru, ka pat tu reiz būsi laimīgs!"
Tur mātes vārdu piemin Mātes dienā,
un gaili Mārtiņos, un olas Lieldienās.

5.

Mēs, veļu laikā ieņemtie uz grīdas puspabeigtā verandā.
Mēs, puspelēkās drēbēs greizā skolas solā.
Kas savas ādas vākos iesien ābeci.
No saviem kauliem izliec savu šūpuli.
Kas visu mūžu neatgriežas tumšā, siltā verandā.

WE

1.

We are not angry with our forbears
who, having propped their rosy apple butts against soft cushions,
stare at the screen grazing peacefully.
Heavy-hearted we sit home at Midsummer
And cannot sleep with all the shrieks and blasts.

2.

We'll see the winter through in warmth and light
collecting sharp and fragile objects here at home.
No unexpected turns, no sudden thrusts –
we slip into each other's dark
to wake amidst sharp shards of rays.

3.

We have no prejudice – just go ahead and marry
that lizard basking in between the shrubs.
Yet mind you – he will come with his old tails,
they'll sit in plastic bags on bookshelves in your home
and thump will go his heart in the pocket of his briefs.

4.

In good health and in life
we are kept through small talk replete with holiday cheer:
"I hope even you will be happy one day!"
Motherfuck they save for Mother's Day,
Cock for St. Martin's, eggs for Easter.

5.

We were conceived on the floor of a veranda half-built.
Clothed in gray, we sit behind warped desks at school.
We bind our ABCs in our own skins
And bend own bones to build our cradles.
We who'll not be back to that warm and dark veranda.

PROBLĒMAS

Riebīgā māksla – no tās nāk vienīgi nepatikšanas. Atveras priekškars. Parādās pirmie kadri. Atšķiru pirmo lappusi. Vienmēr jau skaidrs – būs sūdi.

Manā acu priekšā Otello tic visādām blēņām. Trepļevs murgo. Jūlijas jaunkundze meklē kašķi. Man jau skaidrs – labi tas nebeigsies.

Lapa pēc lapas, cēliens pēc cēliena. Ģimenes idille izjūk. Mīlestība nomirst. Atklājas drausmīgā patiesība. Atskan šāviens. Varone sajūk prātā.

Aizšķiru lappusi. Apturu disku. Ceļos un spraucos ārā no zāles, citiem kāpdams uz kājām. Ieslēdzos dzīvoklī, tumšā istabā guļu zem segas.

Neviens nešauj man logos bultas, nestāv pie durvīm ar koka zirgu, bruņukuģis "Potjomkins" nebrauc pa ielu. Atceros savu mīļāko ainu – monotonai mūzikai skanot, palagos vārtās rožaini ķermeņi, savītām kājām, kunkstēdami. Necieš neviens un nemuld.

REMONTS

Tikai sestdienās, svētdienās un svētku dienās mēs drīkstam gulēt vienā šķirstā – pavērt ķirmju saēstās durvis ar līku, brangu rokturi, elpot viens otra trūdaino dvašu, visu nakti vārtīties pīšļos.

Lai rītā, atgriežoties tur augšā, redzētu – sairusi vēl kāda pussala, nodilis vēl kāds zemesrags, vēl daži mākoņi nokrituši uz zemes, viss aptīts palagiem, pārklājies baltiem pelniem.

Pusdienlaikā ietrīsas zirnekļu tīkli, mēs saņemam ziņas par jaunajām nelaimēm, kas atgadījušās visā pasaulē. Pērkam vīnu, dodamies ciemos pie draugiem.

Pārrunājam dīvainas pašnāvības, īpaši smieklīgas bēru paražas. Dažkārt kāds patēlo beigtu, bet citi stāsta par viņu visjaukākās lietas un bēdā, cik ļoti tā pietrūkst.

Šai sausajā pagrabā, kur stiklos mirdz gurķi un sēnes, šūpojas sīpolu ķēdes un plauktos smaida oranžu ķirbju bezzobu mutes.

PROBLEMS

That disgusting art – all it does is bring problems. The curtain opens. The first frames appear. I open the first page. And it's always clear – some shit will happen.

In front of my very eyes Othello believes in some bullshit. Treplev rants. Miss Julie is picking a fight. I know for sure – no good will come of it.

Page after page, act after act. The family idyll unravels. Love dies. The horrible truth comes out. A shot rings out. The heroine goes mad.

I close the book. I stop the disc. I get up and squeeze out of the audience, stepping on toes. I lock myself up in the apartment, lie down in a dark room under the blanket.

No one shoots arrows at my window, no one stands by my door with a hobby-horse, battleship Potemkin does not float by in the street. I remember my favourite scene – against a background of monotone music, rosy bodies roll around between the sheets, their legs entwined, softly moaning. No one is suffering, no one talks bullshit.

RENOVATION

It is only Saturdays, Sundays and holidays that we can lie in the same casket – open the brittle door with its crooked handle, breathe each other's stale breath, wallow in dust all night long.

So that in the morning, returning up there, we see – another peninsula crumbled, another cape submerged, yet another few clouds fallen to earth, everything swaddled in sheets, covered in pale ash.

At noon the cobwebs are aflutter, we receive news about the latest disasters that have visited various parts of the globe. We buy wine, go visit friends.

We discuss strange suicides, particularly funny funeral customs. Now and then someone pretends to be dead, others tell beautiful stories and say how much he'll be missed.

In this dry cellar where pickles shine behind glass, where strings of onions sway in the breeze and orange pumpkins grin toothless on shelves.

SNIEGAVĪRS

Te nu es stāvu, citādi nevaru, kails tavā priekšā vakara krēslā. Tu mani pats esi izveidojis – bezmiega naktīs, ziemas salā, apķepinādams ar savām siekalām, savām asarām. Ar saviem sviedriem, puņķiem un spermu.

Tu mani veidoji, neveikli glāstot. Te nu es stāvu, liels un dīvains, bālgans un grubuļains tavā priekšā. Saki – vai es tev vēl patīku? Ja kaut kas labojams, atceries – šobrīd vēl ziema, ja gribam būt precīzi – janvāris.

STATUS QUO

Atzīšanās mīlestībā – skaista kā neatkarības pasludināšana. Pēc ilgiem opozīcijā pavadītiem gadiem ievācāmies romantiskā dienesta dzīvoklī – pastalās, respektīvi, pliki – gadiem neizlīdām no cisām. Un ūsainas karalienes atzina mūs *de facto*.

Šodien atkal valsts svētki un salūts, glāzītes mirdz kā ordeņi, uzkodu vietā skūpsti. *Ergo bibamus*, mans princi, mēs nozagām veselu valsti kā tukšu sirdi.

VĒSTULE

Noplēsu kuponus, kopā ar tukšajiem iepakojumiem aizsūtīju aploksnē, taču atbildi nesaņēmu. Nokasīju sudraba joslu, bet skaitlis „10 000" neparādījās. Arī bultas vai sirsniņas attēlu apakš alus korķa neieraudzīju.

Likās, ka visu pareizi daru, bet mana laime, redz, kavējas. Manu vārdu Lieldienu zaķis neizvilka no cepures un nevicināja ķepā pa visu studiju.

Tā nu es sēžu bez ceļojuma uz Alpiem, bez tostera, bez „Narvesen" dāvanu kartes. Pārdevējas klusē kā sfinksas, pastniece noplāta rokas, bet televīzijas telefons vienmēr aizņemts.

Likās, ka visu pareizi daru, visu pareizi atbildēju – gan tēlu grieķu mitoloģijā, gan pasaules čempionu šahā, gan naudas vienību Kazahijā. Kur kavējas mana laime, kur viņas mazās dāvaniņas?

Laikam es esmu pārlieku resns un bāls. Laikam valkāju nesmukas drēbes. Laikam man draugos vien sliņķi un lūzeri. Nenāk Laime ne tuvu pie manas pastkastītes, jo es tajā baroju putniņus.

SNOWMAN

Here I stand, I cannot do otherwise, naked in front of you, under the evening shadows. You shaped me yourself – during sleepless nights, in the dead of winter, smearing me with your saliva, your tears. With your sweat, your snot, and your sperm.

You shaped me, caressing me awkwardly. So here I stand, large and strange, pale and bumpy before your eyes. Tell me – do you still like me? If there's anything that still can be changed, remember: it's still winter, January, to be precise

STATUS QUO

Confession of love – beautiful like a proclamation of independence. After many years spent in opposition, we moved into a romantic company flat – in rags, i.e., naked – and for years did not venture outside. And moustachioed queens recognized us *de facto*.

Today it's the national holiday again, fireworks, glasses sparkle like medals, kisses in place of *hors d'oeuvres*. *Ergo bibamus*, my prince, we stole an entire country like one empty heart.

LETTER

I cut out the coupons, sent them off in an envelope with the empty wrappings enclosed, but got no reply. I scratched at the silver band, but no number "10 000" appeared. And there were no hearts or arrows under the bottle cap.

It seemed I was doing everything right, yet my Fortune was somehow held up. It was not my name the Easter Bunny pulled out of the hat and paraded all over the studio.

So here I am: no trip to the Alps, no toaster, no Narvesen gift certificate. The salesgirls are mute like the Sphinx, the postman shrugs, helpless, and the TV phones are forever busy.

It seemed I was doing everything right, I gave the right answers – named the character from Greek mythology, the world champion in chess, the legal tender in Kazakhstan. Where is my Fortune then, where are her little favours?

I must be too fat and too pale. It must be my ugly clothes. Or it must be my friends, those loafers and losers. Fortune passes my post box by, for I use it to feed little birds.

ZĪMES

Tiklīdz tev kaut kas nepatīk, nekavējoties dod par to zināt – signalizē ar noliektu pieri un samiegtām acīm, neliec man svaidīties šaubās un minējumos.

Lai straujāks galvas pagrieziens vai tikko manāma lūpu drebēšana dod nepārprotamu mājienu – divvientulības planēta briesmās, Mazais Princis veltīgi meklē tās apaļo apvārsni, lai pieķertos, pieturētos, neatkristu tālu melnajās orbītās.

Lai runā sažņaugtās dūres un galvai pārvilktā sega – mans trokšņu slāpētais adresant, mana semiotikas mācību grāmata, atver acis kaut vai uz brīdi, kaut vai parādi mēli.

SIGNS

As soon as you don't like something let me know right away: signal with a lowered brow and squinting eyes, do not let me toss about in self-doubt and guessing.
Let a sudden turn of the head or barely noticeable trembling of lips serve as an explicit hint: the planet of twosomeness is in danger, the Little Prince searching in vain for its round horizon to grasp, to hold on, to prevent himself from falling far back into the black orbits.
Let tightened fists and head hidden under a blanket speak – my noise reduced addressee, my semiotics textbook, open your eyes if for a brief moment, stick out your tongue.

PHOTO: MARC GEBER

IEVA LEŠINSKA-GABER (Ieva Lešinska) was born in 1958, attended secondary school in Riga and went on to study English at the University of Riga. From 1978 to 1987 she lived and worked in the USA, studying at Ohio State University and the University of Colorado, before moving to Sweden in 1987 to work as a freelance journalist and translator, at the same time as following the Master of Arts programme in Baltic Philology at the University of Stockholm.

She now lives in Riga, working as chief translator at the Bank of Latvia, and as a free-lance journalist and translator. She has translated the poetry of Seamus Heaney, Robert Frost, D. H. Lawrence, Ezra Pound, Dylan Thomas, T. S. Eliot and various American Beat Generation poets into Latvian, and has published numerous English translations of poems and prose by Latvian authors in periodicals and anthologies in the UK and the US.

PHOTO: TONY WARD

Juris Kronbergs (b. 1946) is one of the foremost Latvian poets writing also in Swedish. The author of twelve books of poetry, he is also a prolific translator, having rendered many of the most important twentieth- and twenty-first-century Latvian poets into Swedish. His translations from Swedish most notably include the collected poems of Thomas Tranströmer, together with Guntars Godiņš (Riga: Mansards, 2011) and a novel by Ulf Eriksson, *Varelser av glas* (Riga: Jānis Roze, 2010). To the English reader, Kronbergs is probably best known from his cycle of poems *Wolf One-Eye* translated by Mara Rozitis (Todmorden: Arc Publications, 2006), whose original Latvian won him the Latvian Writers' Union Prize of 1997, has been translated into several other languages and issued on CD:s in Latvia and Sweden (musical accompaniment by Kristaps Grasis). Kronbergs' latest collection of poetry was published under the title *Ik diena* (Every Day / Riga: Mansards, 2011).

Other anthologies of poetry in translation published in bilingual editions by Arc Publications include:

Six Slovenian Poets
ED. BRANE MOZETIČ
Translated by Ana Jelnikar, Kelly Lennox Allen & Stephen Watts, with an introduction by Aleš Debeljak
NO. 1 IN THE 'NEW VOICES FROM EUROPE & BEYOND' ANTHOLOGY SERIES, SERIES EDITOR: ALEXANDRA BÜCHLER

Six Basque Poets
ED. MARI JOSE OLAZIREGI
Translated by Amaia Gabantxo, with an introduction by Mari Jose Olaziregi
NO. 2 IN THE 'NEW VOICES FROM EUROPE & BEYOND' ANTHOLOGY SERIES, SERIES EDITOR: ALEXANDRA BÜCHLER

Six Czech Poets
ED. ALEXANDRA BÜCHLER
Translated by Alexandra Büchler, Justin Quinn & James Naughton, with an introduction by Alexandra Büchler
NO. 3 IN THE 'NEW VOICES FROM EUROPE & BEYOND' ANTHOLOGY SERIES, SERIES EDITOR: ALEXANDRA BÜCHLER

Six Lithuanian Poets
ED. EUGENIJUS ALIŠANKA
Various translators, with an introduction by Eugenijus Ališanka
NO. 4 IN THE 'NEW VOICES FROM EUROPE & BEYOND' ANTHOLOGY SERIES, SERIES EDITOR: ALEXANDRA BÜCHLER

Six Polish Poets
ED. JACEK DEHNEL
Various translators, with an introduction by Jacek Dehnel
NO. 5 IN THE 'NEW VOICES FROM EUROPE & BEYOND' ANTHOLOGY SERIES, SERIES EDITOR: ALEXANDRA BÜCHLER

Six Slovak Poets
ED. IGOR HOCHEL
Translated by John Minahane, with an introduction by Igor Hochel
NO. 6 IN THE 'NEW VOICES FROM EUROPE & BEYOND' ANTHOLOGY SERIES, SERIES EDITOR: ALEXANDRA BÜCHLER

Six Macedonian Poets
ED. IGOR ISAKOVSKI
Various translators, with an introduction by Ana Martinoska
NO. 7 IN THE 'NEW VOICES FROM EUROPE & BEYOND' ANTHOLOGY SERIES, SERIES EDITOR: ALEXANDRA BÜCHLER

Altered State: An Anthology of New Polish Poetry
EDS. ROD MENGHAM, TADEUSZ PIÓRO, PIOTR SZYMOR
Translated by Rod Mengham, Tadeusz Pióro *et al.*

A Fine Line: New Poetry from Eastern & Central Europe
EDS. JEAN BOASE-BEIER, ALEXANDRA BÜCHLER, FIONA SAMPSON
Various translators

A Balkan Exchange: Eight Poets from Bulgaria & Britain
ED. W. N. HERBERT

The Page and The Fire: Poems by Russian Poets on Russian Poets
ED. PETER ORAM
Selected, translated and introduced by Peter Oram

More Latvian poetry published by Arc:

Wolf One-Eye
by **JURIS KRONBERGS**
Translated from the Latvian by Mara Rozitis

You may also be interested in:

The Scent of Your Shadow
by **KRISTINA EHIN**
Translated from the Estonian by Ilmar Lehtpere

Shape of Time
by **DORIS KAREVA**
Translated from the Estonian by Tiina Aleman

The Ballads of Kukutis
by **MARCELIJUS MARTINAITIS**
Translated from the Lithuanian by Laima Vincė

Ingram Content Group UK Ltd.
Milton Keynes UK
UKHW012125230323
419066UK00004B/242